NO GREATER

Books by A.W. Tozer

COMPILED AND EDITED BY JAMES L. SNYDER

Alive in the Spirit

And He Dwelt Among Us

A Cloud by Day, a Fire by Night

The Crucified Life

The Dangers of a Shallow Faith

Delighting in God

A Disruptive Faith

The Essential Tozer Collection 3-in-1

Experiencing the Presence of God

God's Power for Your Life

Living as a Christian

My Daily Pursuit

No Greater Love

Preparing for Jesus' Return

The Purpose of Man

The Pursuit of God

The Quotable Tozer

Reclaiming Christianity

Voice of a Prophet

The Wisdom of God

Books by James L. Snyder

The Life of A.W. Tozer: In Pursuit of God—The Authorized Biography

NO GREATER

LOVE

EXPERIENCING
THE HEART OF JESUS
THROUGH THE GOSPEL OF JOHN

A.W. TOZER

COMPILED AND EDITED BY JAMES L. SNYDER

BETHANYHOUSE
a division of Baker Publishing Group
Minneapolis, Minnesota

© 2020 by James L. Snyder

Published by Bethany House Publishers
11400 Hampshire Avenue South
Bloomington, Minnesota 55438
www.bethanyhouse.com

Bethany House Publishers is a division of
Baker Publishing Group, Grand Rapids, Michigan

Printed in the United States of America

Library of Congress Cataloging-in-Publication Data
Names: Tozer, A. W. (Aiden Wilson), 1897-1963, author.
Title: No greater love : experiencing the heart of Jesus through the Gospel of John /
    A.W. Tozer, James L. Snyder.
Other titles: Sermons. Selections
Description: Minneapolis : Bethany House, a division of Baker Publishing Group,
    2019.
Identifiers: LCCN 2019020805 | ISBN 9780764218101 (trade paper) | ISBN
    9781493421787 (e-book)
Subjects: LCSH: Bible. John—Sermons. | Love—Biblical teaching—Sermons.
Classification: LCC BS2615.6.L6 T69 2019 | DDC 252—dc23
LC record available at https://lccn.loc.gov/2019020805

Scripture quotations are from the King James Version of the Bible.

Cover design by Rob Williams, InsideOutCreativeArts

James L. Snyder is represented by The Steve Laube Agency.

24 25 26   7 6 5

In keeping with biblical principles of creation stewardship, Baker Publishing Group advocates the responsible use of our natural resources. As a member of the Green Press Initiative, our company uses recycled paper when possible. The text paper of this book is composed in part of post-consumer waste.

Contents

Introduction

Many of us tend to think of love as a sentimental or emotional thing, not stopping to explore the true depths of it. Perhaps that is why this subject never gets its due coverage. I don't think anybody would ever accuse A.W. Tozer of being sentimental. When he deals with a subject, he takes it right on, face-to-face. I think that is what people like about reading a Tozer book.

Tozer spent over fifty sermons preaching through the gospel of John, and this book presents his insights on God's love for us, drawn from this gospel.

Listening to Tozer preach these sermons is quite an experience. When preaching, Tozer never followed a word-by-word script or even a detailed outline. He would fold a piece of paper in two, put notes on the left-hand side and on the right-hand side, and tuck it into his Bible.

Keep in mind, those notes were carefully and prayerfully prepared. To him, it was almost an act of worship. I have many of his sermon notes and the audio sermons that go with them. It is quite interesting to follow the notes as he is preaching.

Although I say that his notes were somewhat of an "act of worship," he never worshiped the notes. The preparation might have been an act of worship, but the notes themselves were simply a tool to preach a sermon that God would bless.

One of the wonderful things to me about listening to Tozer's sermons is the rabbit trails he often took. He would be going down one line of thought and, out of thin air, would seemingly change topics. More often than not, those rabbit trails are fascinating, and many are included in this book.

When preaching, Tozer was not glued to his notes. He was concerned about allowing the Holy Spirit to lead him in the delivery of that message. If it involved rabbit trails, that was good enough for him.

In this book, I have tried to keep the feel of a sermon. Not an essay in itself, but a sermon that would emphasize Tozer's real commitment to the Lord Jesus Christ.

I believe the title *No Greater Love* solidifies what Tozer is saying. In fact, his treatment of John 3:16 is most interesting. These sermons were being preached toward the latter part of his life, and what he says about John 3:16 reveals Tozer's character and nature.

He testifies that he had never before preached on this one verse in his entire ministry. He had quoted it when preaching and also in his prayers, but he had never focused a sermon on that one verse. It is clear that John 3:16 was so important to him, and Tozer carried with him a burden of God's love in his life.

One phrase Tozer uses that is so powerful is "I am the most important person in God's eyes." What a powerful statement.

We like to say that God loves everybody. However, Tozer points out that God does not focus on groups of people, but rather on individuals. God sees the individual and treats them as though they were the only one in the world.

After listening to that sermon, I had to stop and think about that. It took me several days before I could get back to working on this manuscript. I do not think many people really appreciate the love that God has for us, and we take for granted what it really means.

In reading this book, you will see that Tozer came at this subject from a variety of ways. I believe the more you get into this book, the more you will be fascinated by the awesomeness of God's love and how that love is channeled individually.

There are times when Tozer is rather harsh, especially toward religion. He says the problem with Christianity today is that the Pharisees are running it. Pharisees, especially in Jesus' day, were more interested in law than they were in love. They would put law upon law upon law until the weight of the whole thing came crashing down on the hearts of the people.

Very strongly, Tozer puts these religious leaders in their place. He firmly believed that the laws of religion were really keeping people from experiencing the love of God.

He agreed that those Pharisees could explain and talk about it for days on end, defining it in the most intimate way. The problem, as Tozer saw it, was they believed in God's love but had never experienced it themselves. That is the problem with religion today.

We can explain everything in the Bible, but we have yet to experience the truth in the Word of God. This was Tozer's passion: It does no good to know the truth unless you also have experienced the truth.

Another interesting element of this book is Tozer's discussion of the unpardonable sin in one chapter. Not too many people talk about this. Those who do talk about it often seem to misunderstand. Tozer gives a wonderful definition of the unpardonable sin and how we as Christians today can deal with it. If we do not know what it is and how it affects us, it will damage and compromise Christianity for us.

My greatest challenge in putting this book together was deciding what not to include. These sermons on the gospel of John are some of the best of Tozer's. Because he was coming to the end of his ministry in Chicago, he poured into each sermon wisdom he received from God along with the illumination of the Holy Spirit.

Some may not agree with everything Tozer says here—Tozer himself would not want them to—but going through this book and thinking through it chapter by chapter will point you in the right direction.

I suggest you read one chapter and then think about what you just read. Reading a Tozer book is not a competition to see how fast you can read it. It is experiencing the truth as he experienced it, and you will come away different than when you started.

James L. Snyder

1

Christ's Focused Love

O Father, the love of Christ is the most amazing thing that I could ever experience. I praise Thee Christ has focused His love on me and brought me into Thy kingdom. May my life daily give testimony of Thy love. Amen.

Marvel not that I said unto thee, Ye must be born
again.

—John 3:7

Sometimes we can go too far and exaggerate, making statements by using a superlative. However, it is
quite difficult to exaggerate the vital importance of
the teaching of our Lord in the opening verses of John 3. It
is wholly revolutionary.

It is sharply classifying; it excludes and includes, it divides
and distinguishes human beings from each other. It differs
from all other religious teaching and is more than religious
teaching. It did not originate with the teacher. It is not a pat-
tern of truth woven out of many threads, as most religious
teaching is. It is not anything like that.

Simply put, it is practical reporting.

When a reporter goes out on assignment, he sends back
what he has seen and heard. We do not consider it the teaching of that reporter. We simply say it is factual reporting.

This is what Jesus is doing: "Verily, verily, I say unto thee, We speak that we do know, and testify that we have seen; and ye receive not our witness" (John 3:11).

Here, Jesus takes on himself the character of a reporter, and to put it in language we understand, He says, "I am reporting to you what I know and have seen." This is not pieced-out teaching—it is reporting. It is a report to men on earth of what He, the Lord of heaven, saw and heard and knew while He was in heaven. "And no man hath ascended up to heaven, but he that came down from heaven, even the Son of man which is in heaven" (v. 13).

Jesus understood that many people would not accept his report: "If I have told you earthly things, and ye believe not, how shall ye believe, if I tell you of heavenly things? And no man hath ascended up to heaven, but he that came down from heaven, even the Son of man which is in heaven" (vv. 12–13).

That was his explanation when Nicodemus asked, "How can these things be?" (v. 9).

Jesus says people will not believe what He is telling them or what He saw. They will even reject it. There are two main reasons behind this.

First, people love the earth and sin too much, and second, they have no confidence in the One who is reporting. It is simply unbelief in the Savior, the Son of God.

Unbelief is not a weakness or failure of the mind. Rather, it is an opinion. When we do not believe in Jesus, we have an opinion of Jesus, which prevents us from believing.

A reporter goes to Washington, DC, and writes what he saw and heard. We sometimes shrug off his story not because we are unable to understand it, nor because we have some psychological weakness. It is simply because we have no confidence in the reporter.

There are those who accept that God is true when they believe His message. But there are those who deny that God is true, or at least that Jesus Christ is God's Son, and they doubt the veracity of the reporter and refuse to accept the record.

What is it that our Lord is saying?

There are basic contrasts emphasized here by our Savior and taught by the apostles elsewhere in the Bible.

First, there are two heads of the human race. There is the first Adam, the head of the natural race, the forefather of us all but in whom all have died. As 1 Corinthians 15:22 says, "For as in Adam all die, even so in Christ shall all be made alive."

Then there is Christ, the last Adam, the head of the redeemed human race, and we read about Him in many places, such as 1 Corinthians 15:44–45: "It is sown a natural body; it is raised a spiritual body. There is a natural body, and there is a spiritual body. And so it is written, the first man Adam was made a living soul; the last Adam was made a quickening spirit."

There you have the contrast between the two heads of the human race. Adam, the head of the natural race, and Christ, the head of the spiritual human race, for He was and is a quickening spirit. "The first man is of the earth, earthy; the second man is the Lord from heaven" (v. 47).

These two human races are coexisting and comingling. The ones that belong to the first Adam are human beings everywhere, and the ones belonging to the other are the new ones created in Christ Jesus unto good works. "If any man be in Christ," Paul tells us in 2 Corinthians 5:17, "he is a new creature," and thus he has a new head, which is Jesus Christ the Lord. Adam is no longer his head. He does not go back to Adam; he goes back to Christ. He does not take his life from Adam; he takes his life from Christ and gets his likeness from Christ. Christ is the new head of the new creation and of those who are born of the Spirit.

Here is where the real trouble begins; these two human races coexist in the world. That is the reason for persecution and religious trouble in every city.

This comingling and coexisting is seen in the fact that redeemed people live in cities, eat food, go to work, drive automobiles, talk on telephones, pay bills, and do everything that the old Adam's race does. But, lo and behold, the mystery of mysteries, something wonderful has happened to that one group. They look like the others, but they are not like them. They can hardly be distinguished, but they are different from the others in that though they are born of Adam's seed they have been rescued from Adam's seed and born into the kingdom of God. That leads us to the two kingdoms coexisting: the kingdom of the flesh and the kingdom of the Spirit, which is also called the kingdom of God.

I believe in the brotherhood of man. I believe there is a universal brotherhood of the once born, and then I believe in a universal brotherhood of the twice born. Where our modernistic and liberal friends make their mistake is that they do not distinguish between the once born and the twice born. They make a universal brotherhood and say everybody is in. Jesus Christ makes a universal brotherhood and says everybody is out except those who are born again. The liberal might say, "I believe in the brotherhood of man and that all in the universal brotherhood are children of God." Jesus says there is a universal brotherhood of the flesh: "Jesus answered, Verily, verily, I say unto thee, Except a man be born of water and of the Spirit, he cannot enter into the kingdom of God. That which is born of the flesh is flesh; and that which is born of the Spirit is spirit" (John 3:5–6).

I believe in the universal brotherhood of fallen man and in the fatherhood of God.

Not the fatherhood of God over the whole race of Adam, for that is not so. Rather, the fatherhood of God over them born anew, who are saved. Christians have God for a father. The man in the old world was born of Adam and has Adam for his father, not God. God created Adam, Adam had progeny, the whole world is populated by the progeny of Adam, and our universal brothers descended from one ancient father, but not so with the children of God.

When we enter the kingdom of God, we become children of the Most High, and then we enter this new brotherhood of the redeemed, of whom God is the Father and Jesus Christ is the head.

There are two kingdoms; the kingdom of the flesh is inhabited by Adam's descendants. The human race is united by blood and common origin, and as we see it scattered over the world it is separated by color and language. They are sons of Adam, all of one blood, and they inhabit the face of the earth.

There are differences on the cultural level, on the educational level, and in the advancements of scientific achievement and degrees of civilization. There is what they called the Stone Age, when the only weapons and machinery they had were made of stones. Then came the age of steel. Now we come to the age of the atom, but it is all Adam's race nevertheless.

He can ride in a plane or in a wheelbarrow; it is the same old son of Adam. He is just the same even though he has improved over what he was before. There are differences among the sons of Adam, but they are all one in that they inhabit the kingdom of the flesh.

Then there is the kingdom of the Spirit, which is sometimes referred to as the kingdom of God and is inhabited by the Spirit-born people. They are separated just as we have separation in Adam's kingdom, the kingdom of the flesh, which is separated by language and color and so on. Therefore, we have in the kingdom of God certain separations too.

We are divided by language barriers and distance, which keep God's people apart.

On the day of Pentecost, they were all of one accord in one place. That would be impossible today to get all the church together in one place—there are simply too many of us. No stadium in the world is big enough to hold all the redeemed people of God; a company no man can number, you cannot get them into one space. It is impossible to get all of God's people together, and furthermore, we do not live together in time. Some are already dead; some have been dead a long time; some Christians are not yet born; so there is a time division and a space separation.

We also have little incidental separations.

For instance, a born-again Lutheran was brought up as a Christian in the Lutheran church and by a certain narrow, limited view of things does not know there are any other kinds of Christians. And a Baptist in the South says, "I never have gone to any other church in my life except a Baptist church." He just does not know what he is missing.

Then we have the kingdom of the Spirit. Some say all Christians are supposed to be together in one denomination. Divisions are terrible between Christians, but it's impossible not to have some disagreements. We are scattered all over the face of the earth. But in spite of those temporary and surface separations we're all one, united by birth out of one Spirit, baptized into one Spirit, members in one body with one Father and one Savior and one Lord and one Bridegroom and one heaven toward which we are moving.

Instead of sneering at the hymn that says, "We are not divided. All one body we," let us just thank God it is true. Let us thank God that it's true and that there is a kingdom composed of those who belong to the spiritual world, and they are all one, undivided, and Jesus said that they all may be one and so we are, just as the human race is one.

We have two kingdoms and two births. What does Jesus say about that which is born of the flesh?

That which is born of the flesh can never be anything but flesh and can never cross over into the kingdom of the Spirit on its own. All the religious education you can get will not enable you to cross over into the kingdom of the Spirit. All of the disciples' teaching and instruction and education will not make Spirit followers out of us.

We have all the reasoning of a Plato; flesh still remains flesh. We have all the art of a Michelangelo; flesh is still flesh. We have all the music of a Beethoven; flesh is still flesh. Though we have the genius of an Einstein, flesh is still flesh. That which is born of the flesh is flesh, and you cannot by any means known to mortal man bring the flesh across into the Spirit's kingdom.

There is the birth that makes us flesh, puts us in the body of Adam, and makes us inhabitants of the kingdom of Adam. There is also a birth, which is of the Spirit, that puts us into the kingdom of God and makes God our father and Christ our head. That which is born of the flesh remains flesh, and that which is of the Spirit has another destiny altogether.

The destiny of the twice born is eternal life in heaven presided over by the Lord of life and surrounded by the light of God. This is the destiny of the twice born.

I must understand that there are those who are of old Adam, brothers in a fallen race; Scripture says shame and everlasting contempt is theirs in the day when they rise from the dust of the earth. They who now inhabit the old kingdom have the money, have a good bit of education, and usually run things, but these are the sons of Adam.

We just have to wait until the day when God will judge the heart of every man by His gospel, but in the meantime, we are living in another world. We live on two levels at once: the level of Adam and the level of Christ. We were born up into another level, the level of the Spirit, and there we meet and mingle with all the good saints down the years. I believe in the communion of saints, as the Apostles' Creed says. It means that I have a level in my life where I am one with all who have gone before me.

I must understand that if I am in the kingdom of God rather than the kingdom of the world, the focus of Christ's love is on me. Those in the kingdom of the world cannot accept or appreciate the love Christ has for them.

In this kingdom of God, I have the ability to receive from Christ the love He has for me. I must understand that the focus of all of God's love is on His people, because they are the ones who can receive it and believe it.

2

Christ's Emotional Love

O heavenly Father of my Lord and Savior Jesus Christ, how my heart rejoices in the love Thou hast for me through Jesus. Thank Thee for that love, and help me, O God, to embrace that love in every aspect of my life. In the wonderful name of Jesus I pray, amen.

For God so loved the world, that he gave his only begotten son, that whosoever believeth in him should not perish, but have everlasting life.

—John 3:16

I think I would be safe in saying that John 3:16 is probably the most popular verse in the entire Bible. More people know this verse than any other verse you could ever mention.

Upon my conversion, I read this verse, and it has been tumbling in my brain ever since. I cannot seem to get away from it. Something in it whets my appetite for the things of God.

But I need to clarify something here. Just because somebody knows something, it does not mean they have experienced it. For example, a person may know John 3:16, but that does not mean they understand it and have embraced it and experienced it. It is the experiencing of John 3:16 that brings life into true spiritual perspective.

I also need to point out that if we did not have the Old Testament, we could not understand what John 3:16 is all about. *Who is this God? Who is His Son?* None of this would be understood if we did not have all of the Bible. You cannot pull a verse out of context and understand its significance.

There will be times as you read through the Bible that a verse will jump out and say things to you and minister to you in ways that you did not think possible. I think John 3:16 can do that sort of thing. It reveals to us the emotional aspect of God's love.

Many do not think that God has emotions. Yet if you look throughout the Scriptures, you will find that God expresses himself in a variety of emotional ways. God does have emotions. He is a personality, and personalities have emotions. So when we speak of God's emotional love, we need to understand several aspects about it.

John 3:16 begins by saying, "For God so loved." This is a very significant beginning. How do you measure the phrase "so loved"? We sometimes measure God's love from our perspective. We could love this situation or this person. We could not love that person or that situation.

However, when we come to God, we find an emotional love that overcomes every obstacle. The Bible says in Acts 10:34, "God is no respecter of persons." That means God does not treat one person differently than He treats another person. God respects people because He created them in His image. The thing we really need to get ahold of is that because God created us in His image, we are the target of His emotional love.

To understand this, I also need to realize that no sin in my life can intimidate God's love. My sin does not overwhelm the love of God. Rather, the love of God overwhelms my sin. That is why John wrote, "If we confess our sins, he is faithful and just to forgive us our sins, and to cleanse us from all unrighteousness" (1 John 1:9).

There is no sin that is too much for God to handle. And I believe I would be correct to say that God's love is individualized. In other words, it is not a group kind of expression. Rather, God's love flows into individual hearts. By that, I simply mean every person has equal access to God's love, and that is Jesus Christ. He is the great equalizer.

"For God so loved the world, that he gave his only begotten Son." This is the path to experiencing God's love. Nothing else. I cannot work my way into the love of God. I cannot charm my way into the love of God. However, I can come into the love of God through that wonderful door, Jesus Christ. "I am the way, the truth, and the life," Jesus said (John 14:6). Therefore, God's love is available to every person individually.

When I read this verse and realize the love that is being demonstrated here, I begin to understand the passion and power of the Deity. Sometimes we have an idea that God is this big mean guy in the sky who wants to stomp on us. That is no picture of God. Neither is He "the man upstairs" who likes me. Rather, when I think of God, especially through John 3:16, I begin to see the tears and the pain that God has experienced because of man.

When God looks at humanity and sees the depravity and the sin, certainly there is pain, and certainly there are tears. That is why God sent His Son, so that we might be able to receive the emotional love that He has for us—and this love cannot be compromised, because nothing can overcome the power and passion of our God.

Now, this emotional love goes two ways. Number one, it is God's love for us. I am not sure that we really comprehend the magnitude of His love. It is everlasting, eternal, without limits. And the thing that God loves the most in all of the universe is the man He created in His own image. So God's love for us has that emotional aspect, that passion. God desires us more than anything else.

Then, of course, there is the other side of the picture: God's anger toward the rebellious. Those who reject God will not experience the love of God, and the vacuum left by that rejection may be filled with the anger of God. God desires us to come to Him, but the rebellious nature of man pushes God away and can only be dealt with through repentance and confession. It does not matter how deep we fall, or how much we sin, the only thing that matters is if we repent and confess that God is emotionally connected to us in such a way that He can forgive us and cleanse us from all unrighteousness.

It is important to understand that God's love for us is rooted in His image. Not in ours. God's love flows out of His nature and His character.

I often do not like someone because of some of the things they do. Sometimes I judge people because they do not measure up to my standard. However, God overrides all of that. His emotional love for me overcomes any obstacle, and if I allow God to come into my life through Jesus Christ, I will experience the dynamics of that love that will transform me step by step into the image of God. That is the purpose of all of this love.

What the devil tried to take away from God, God is more than able to restore to His delight and pleasure.

God delights in us, and His whole love is focused on us. And if that is not emotional, I do not know what it is.

Some people think about emotional love as something that goes up and down, back and forth, and finally crashes at some point. That is not what I mean here. God's love has so much passion and power in it that it overrides common thinking. I cannot think my way into God's presence. It is the love of God that overwhelms me and opens up the gate into His presence. God's great delight is to overcome our depravity. As bad as we are, we are not too bad for God to deliver us from that depravity and bring us into the brightness of His delight.

We also need to understand that God's love never changes. It is a growing love, but that growth is only from our perspective. God never changes in anything. Jesus Christ is the same yesterday and today and forever. Therefore, God does not change, but we do. It is the power of God's emotional love that begins to change us and develop us and cause us to grow in the knowledge of the Lord Jesus Christ.

When we come to Christ, we begin to experience His love. In that very first moment, we have all of God's love, but the problem is, we can only understand so much. But as we continue to follow Him, we begin to understand more and more of what His love is all about. His love is not just a one-time thing: *"Yes, God loves me, and so now I'm going to go off to heaven."* There is a growth there, and the growth leads to understanding more and more what it means to have God's love in my life to the point where I am more and more able to access God's love in my life.

The devil wants me to go around and pout in some corner somewhere, and he tells me that I am not worthy of anything.

All right, you are not worthy of anything, and neither am I. However, our worthiness is not the issue here. It is the worthiness of God and His emotional love that really make the way.

If I had to rest upon my worthiness, I would not get anywhere. But if I rest upon the worthiness of God to love me, I will go into His presence. That is what makes the Christian life so wonderful, to understand that God's love flows from His worthiness, and He is not coming into my life, but rather He is bringing me into His presence to enjoy His strength and grace day by day.

I say "emotional love" because it is a growing thing with me. The more I know about God, the more I want to know about God. And as I begin to experience His love, I begin to see levels of His love that I did not notice before. I begin to see that God's love is bigger than anything I could ever imagine. As I begin to see how big this love of God is, I begin to experience that love in my own life.

I believe one of the bottom-line truths is simply this: If God can love me, and if God can accept my love for Him, then I can love anybody in the world. That is what God wants to do. He wants to pour into my life this emotional love that has no boundaries—that flows back to Him and then flows out to people around me. I can love people who do not deserve my love because I have a God who has loved me even though I did not deserve His love. Once I get a handle on that, I begin to understand John 3:16.

I have looked at this verse all my life and quoted it in many sermons and articles that I have written. Until recently, though, I have never preached a whole sermon on John 3:16. This verse is so magnificent in many regards, and the more I look at it, the more magnificent it becomes. The more magnificent it becomes in my heart and mind, the more I appreciate the love that God has for me. "For God so loved the world, that he gave his only begotten Son, that whosoever believeth in him should not perish, but have everlasting life." The beginning of that everlasting life is experiencing this emotional love that God has for me.

I know who God is only because I have accepted His love on His conditions. I think it is very important to understand God does not send His love on our conditions, but rather He has set the conditions, and the epitome of those conditions is Jesus Christ our Savior. If I am going to experience God's love, it will be through Jesus Christ. That is what love is all about, and again, God's love never changes. His love does not get worse or better or more or less. God's love is the same, and I begin to experience more and more of that love on a daily basis.

Our message to others in the world is that God loves them. Most of religion says that God will love you if you do this and that and do not do this or that. That is not how God operates. God says, "I love you so much that I sent My Son to die for you so you could experience My love for you."

3

Christ's Unconditional Love

Dear heavenly Father, Thine unconditional love to me as a person is mysterious to me. Thank Thee that Thou thought me worthy of Thy love, and I accept it in the name of the Lord Jesus Christ, my Savior. Amen.

For God sent not his Son into the world to condemn the world; but that the world through him might be saved.

—John 3:17

I believe it is hard for us to believe in unconditional love, especially from God's side of the issue.

We always place conditions upon our love. We might say that our love is unconditional, but if something unexpected happens, all of a sudden that love can disappear.

Christ can offer unconditional love because He is all-wise. He knows everything from the beginning to the end. Nothing can ever happen in my life that will ever surprise God. And because of that knowledge, He has offered to me His unconditional love.

Christ came into the world, and the purpose of His coming into the world is for us to know His love in a way that will delight us in God's presence. The purpose is to understand who Christ really is.

You cannot understand who Christ is if you do not have a grasp of what this unconditional love is all about.

The first part of John 3:17 simply says, "For God sent not his Son into the world to condemn the world." This is a very important thing to understand. Many religions these days teach that God is here to condemn us. If some catastrophe happens, people will immediately say God is judging that family, that person, or even that town.

The simple fact is, God is not here to judge the world. The things that are happening in our lives and in the world are the consequences of choices we make. God does not want us to make those choices, but He will not keep us from making them. God's love is not dependent upon the choices we make.

We must understand God, and when we understand God, we will begin to see that Christ did not come to condemn us. If Christ came to condemn us, none of us would survive. Nothing in our lives would entice God to forgive us and to forget all of our sins.

The problem is this: God, being who He is, cannot forget any of our sins, and only through the blood of Jesus Christ can our sins be eternally taken away from our lives. When Christ comes into my life, God looks at me and does not see my past; all He sees is that delightful reflection of His Son, the Lord Jesus Christ.

Some people have a wrong understanding of what salvation is all about. They believe salvation is just something to keep us from going to hell. Well, I suppose it does do that, but if that is your idea of what salvation is, you have completely missed the mark. Salvation is not to save us from something. It is to save us unto something. We are to be saved unto Christ and to encounter His unconditional love in our lives.

When I say that Christ's love is unconditional, I mean it is the same for everyone. God does not treat anybody differently than you or me. We are all the same, and sin is sin no matter how we define it. So Christ comes with His unconditional love that cannot be challenged on any side of the issue.

Of course, we can reject this love. It seems to me that the most terrible time a person who has lived a "good" life could have would be to meet Christ face-to-face and for Him to say those terrible words, "Depart from me, for I never knew you." At that time, the person will see the love that God had for them that they rejected for all eternity. They will be haunted by that rejection.

There is completely no reason to reject the love of God. If you read what it is all about, if you read the Scriptures, if you understand what Christ is talking about, there is no way under the sun that anybody would reject this unconditional love. This love is genuine. It is like choosing between a wooden nickel and a gold bar. Why is it that so many people take the wooden nickel and reject the gold bar?

I think the enemy has clouded our understanding of God and His love for us. It is not God's delight to see us reject His love. I accept this love. Not because I deserve it, but because God deserves for me to come into His abundant love.

The second part of John 3:17 says, "But that the world through him might be saved."

Every road leads to heaven, as far as some people are concerned. But if you think through that idea logically, it does not make sense. Not every road will lead me to Chicago or to New York City. There is one distinctive road to heaven, and that is the Lord Jesus Christ. And the train that gets me from here to heaven is the unconditional love that Christ has for me. Once I am on board that train, nothing else seems to matter. The rejoicing of my heart is not in what I do for the Lord, but rather what He has already done for me and continues to do in me and for me day after day. The thing we need to understand is simply that God desires the whole world to be saved. It is not His pleasure to see any person miss heaven because of rebellion and sin. God's desire is to see everybody be saved and go to heaven. The problem is, not everybody desires to go to heaven.

I know there are people who talk about going to heaven, but if they really understood what heaven was all about, they would be amazed, yet probably not interested in going there. Heaven has nothing to do with you and me. It has everything to do with Christ. And as soon as my life begins to be Christ-focused and that focus continues, I am being prepared for heaven.

When unrepentant gangsters and murderers and the like die, I have heard some of their families say they are now in heaven where they belong. I do not want to contradict anybody, but that is a sad thing to say. It's a sad thing to believe, because the person had nothing in their life to suggest a spirit of repentance and they missed the train to heaven, the unconditional love of Christ.

This unconditional love is not negotiable. God established this love before the foundations of the world were set. Nothing has changed in God's mind that would in any way cause Him to modify this love.

Is not that what religion is all about? Getting together to modify what we believe to try to bring it up to the standard of the culture around us? We come together and have panel discussions so that we can come to an agreement on what something really means. Well, that does not work when it comes to the love of God.

The love of God is not open for panel discussion. Nothing is going to change the love God has for us.

All I need to do is come to God on His terms, and that is confessing the Lord Jesus Christ as my Savior. This love makes every person equal.

We do not like that. We look at people and we see race, gender, and all sorts of other things. But when God looks at people, He sees the image of God. And if a person is not a Christian, that image has been marred and destroyed. The passion of God's heart is to have that image restored through the love of Jesus Christ.

I think all the discrimination today is the work of the enemy to hinder certain people from receiving God's love.

Even though this love is unconditional, we need to understand that when God created man He gave us the power of choice. God will never force anybody into His love. I am going to heaven—not because I die. I am going to heaven because I have accepted the Lord Jesus Christ and I have allowed His love to flow into my heart and overwhelm me with desire and adoration for Him.

When our missionaries go overseas, they often spend the first part of their time there learning the local language. Then they begin to preach the gospel. What they preach is the same gospel that Paul the apostle preached in his time and that we are preaching here in America. The gospel does not change, because God does not change. The unconditional love that God has poured out on us never changes. I might see myself changing as I experience this love, but the love of

God never changes. It is perfect. It is pure. It is holy. And all that means is that God's love does not lack anything at all.

My commitment to Christ is the first stage. This gets me on that love train and enables me to begin experiencing the magnificent love of the Lord Jesus Christ. My commitment to Christ is the important issue.

God's love in my life is not based upon my ability to do things. That seems to be the attitude many people have. They believe God loves them because they do things for Him. That is man's attitude, not God's attitude.

God loves me because He created me in His image, and that is the end of it. I do not bring anything except God's love for me. The only thing I need to do is obey Christ and surrender to His Word. That brings into my life all of the resources of God's love that I need. Day by day and step by step I am experiencing this unconditional love.

I am so amazed by how much God loves me. There are times that I have to stop what I am doing and just meditate upon the wonderful love of Christ in my life. I know I do not deserve it. And the more I do not deserve it, the more the love flows into my life. I know God deserves to love me. That is why He created me. But when it comes to me, I am the most important person in God's eyes.

That is how God feels about every person. God feels about me like He feels about you. And how God feels about you is how He feels about everybody else. Again, God's love comes to me individually. It is not a package deal that we have to get together for. It is an individual acceptance of Christ's love in my life.

I often get weary of the religion that seems to be so prominent today in Christianity. Religion does not seem to help us very much. It only confuses us and adds laws, regulations, and rituals. But there are times that I can get alone with God and meditate upon Him and think about Him and open up my heart and let God overwhelm me with His presence. I do not think there is anything more important in my life than experiencing the presence of God. If I follow Him, I will have all the love I need to live a life that will honor and glorify Him.

I am not out to impress anybody. I am not tempted to impress my family or my friends. I am not tempted to impress the religious community. I am just overwhelmed by the fact that God's love flows unconditionally into my life.

4

Christ's Absolute Love

O God my Father, I bless Thy name. I pray Thou wouldest help me to love Thy name and follow whithersoever Thou goest. I praise Thee with yearning and longing. I open wide the gates of my soul and receive the Lord Jesus Christ and rest in Him and trust Him to take me out of the valley into Thy wonderful presence. I pray this in Jesus' name, amen.

He that cometh from above is above all: he that is of the earth is earthly, and speaketh of the earth: he that cometh from heaven is above all.

—John 3:31

Today, two self-contradictory ideas are being presented. Very often we are reminded that our knowledge and education are much superior to that of the New Testament Christians. Then, we are told we must furnish people of today with a lighter diet because we must make religion attractive and easy in order that it may be palatable for these intellectual giants who tread here today.

People of today, they tell us, simply will not take heavy stuff. But strangely, they are also better educated than people back then and have more knowledge. Yet, do you know that the New Testament, deep and solemn as it is, was written for plain and mostly uneducated believers? Our Lord spoke His wonderful message to many thousands of people who could not read or write and had little.

All they had was what had been written of the Bible. They had no painless method of getting religion. Nobody had fixed it so that they did not have to think. No simplified, streamlined messages or methods were being used or given, and they were expected to understand such books as the book of Romans. They were expected to read 1 John and understand and relish that epistle. They were expected to read the book of Hebrews and understand it. They were expected to read the gospel of John and understand and love and relish and live by it.

Now we are being told today that we cannot give people heavy stuff such as this. We must come down to their level and have it streamlined and put in fiction form so the people of today will get it.

The simple truth is, the modern revolt against serious truth with its corresponding demand for streamlined religion is not the result of intellectual deficiency. It is the result of carnality and a lack of spiritual appetite.

I just wonder how long God's people are going to limp along or ride on the coattails of teachers who are petering out. They never get on the coattails of a fellow who is on the upswing but always on those of one who is coming down so that now we are fictioneers. We must put it in story form, they say.

《《《《《○》》》》》

So what is John saying in John 3:31? "He that is of the earth is earthly."

Humanity has fallen into a great deep valley, and all around us are seismic cliffs. In that valley are clouds, casting a shadow of death over everything.

That is the fall of man, which is where we find ourselves. No one has a ladder to get out, and no one can climb out or help another because we are all down here together. How to get out and get back into the sunshine where there is light, nobody knows, for we are all fallen together.

Down in this valley where we find ourselves, some are taller than others and stand up and make others look short by comparison. However, when two men are reaching for the stars and one is a little taller than the other, there is no advantage. One man might be six feet four and the other four feet six, but when they stand up on a hill and reach for the stars, the heavens above smile, because neither one will get close.

Everything in this world is on a horizontal plane, a level; we are all here together. Every time the earthly man opens his mouth he talks like a man of the earth; he's earthly, and those who know God can detect the smell of the burnt earth upon him. If a man rises to help another, he comes to the other one on a horizontal plane. He comes over to the man and tries to help him, but because of his own limitations, he cannot help the other one up.

We find earthly people everywhere around us. Newspapers are filled with earthly minded writings. Magazines vie with each other to entertain us—earthly people entertaining earthly people. Earthly people talk to earthly people about earthly things, and the light above is out, and the mud beneath our feet gives way to the fact that we are fallen. The sunshine and the silver clouds are not ours. We are doomed to walk in the valley; and the pit into which we have fallen is a pit of sin.

Human reason cannot save us, simply because human reason is fallen. That which is fallen cannot raise itself above its fallen level, and human reason is fallen like the human body and the human soul are fallen. Human reason extends out from its fallen level to another man on the fallen level and entertains him with high ideals, but it cannot lift him out of the clay. It cannot fly him out of that low, cloud-covered valley. It cannot take him out of its shadow.

A man can sit down like a thinker and think until his hair is gray, and when he gets up and shakes himself he is still where he was before. He is not out of the valley. He is still behind the sheer walls, but He who comes from above is above human reason, and He never learned or gained anything from it, nor does He owe anything to it or take any advantage from it or have any need of it. He who comes from above is unique.

He who comes from above is incarnated reason. The old theologians said that one of the attributes of God is reason. That little bit of reason you and I have is fallen and broken like a shattered vase. The little bit you and I can gather up, scrape the mud off of, polish, and send to school, that is a bit of shattered reason, which was given us of God, who is the fountain and source of all reason.

A man talks about his reason, and yet human reason cannot get him out. You cannot reason yourself up a sheer wall, and you cannot reason yourself out of the pit, because your human reason is fallen and subject to error. He comes down; He is the incarnation of reason.

He who comes from above is above human science, and human science is nothing but the application of reason to matter and natural laws. We are terribly frightened today because of the existence of things like the hydrogen bomb, which could be more devastating than anything we've seen before. I do not know how far science is going to take us.

Then I think of human civilization. What is human civilization? It is simply education, science, and art applied to the task of refining people and making them more comfortable in the valley. That is all.

Then we have human religion, which takes in all religions except the religion of Him who is from above, and it is built out of the bricks made from the bloody mud of the valley in which we find ourselves. We have done pretty well at refining things. Instead of having just an ordinary time, now we have a golden basket that we call religion. And men step into that golden basket. They readily take hold of the side and pull as best they can but do not rise one inch from the bloody mud of the valley. Religion cannot help us. Religion is horizontal. It comes to us from somebody else who teaches us from where they are and where we are, but there is nothing great, nothing elevated, nothing to look to. It is all horizontal.

You can study the religions of the world all you want to, simply getting a little help from the man who is down as far as you are, maybe just a little taller than you.

Jesus Christ is from above, above all reason, all science, all civilization. We know why He said what He said, that the "Father loveth the Son, and hath given all things into his hand" (John 3:35). We know why He said the testimony of the Son is final, and we know why He said he who believes in the Son has everlasting life. The Son brings help from above.

He brought to us the message of God about the many mansions of the redeemed and the just spirits of just men made perfect. He told us of eternal life. He came down, and he who receives Him has everlasting life and he who believes upon Him has eternal life. We see now also why he who does not obey the Son, death remains on him and he's doomed to the valley, and the wrath of God remains on him because he has despised Him who came from above.

I know I sound old-fashioned and I suppose I could be counted radical by some, but with great calmness and insight I am able to tell you that Jesus Christ is enough for you.

What can religion bring me except to comfort me and cheer me a little about being here in the mud? Only one can help us. No one understands our grief.

The world blossoms out with books on how to get peace of mind and peace of soul and peace of this and of that, but when it's all over, it's just a piece of mud and human effort, and it's not God and it's not eternal life and it's not Him who comes from above.

God can save you and bless you right where you are now. He can take you up and give you the essence and foretaste of that eternal life which is of the Father.

As Christians, we do not need to go around apologizing for Christ. We do not need to worry because we cannot make His doctrines fit into what we learned in school. All you learned in school was one fallen head instructing another fallen head. Some of it is true, and some of it is false. Some of it is all mixed up, because it came from one fallen person instructing another who were on the same muddy floor.

What we have in Christ is certainly infinitely superior to the low views we have now. Those are, "I accept Christ in order to escape the atom bomb," "I accept Christ in order that my business might prosper," "I accept Christ for some other low reason."

We accept Christ and know that the Spirit is within us, and we are born into the new world and have help from above.

5

Christ's Contagious Love

Gracious heavenly Father, Thy love is beyond comprehension but not beyond my reception. Thank Thee for love that has become contagious in my own life. In Jesus' name, amen.

Jesus answered and said unto her, If thou knewest the gift of God, and who it is that saith to thee, Give me to drink; thou wouldest have asked of him, and he would have given thee living water.

—John 4:10

Jesus' meeting with the woman at the well is the most fascinating event in His life and ministry. He had good reason not to meet with her. In fact, it was pretty much against the religious law for a Jew to encounter a Samaritan, especially a woman.

It is easy to see why Jesus orchestrated this encounter. Looking at it from our position, it is an example of Christ's contagious love. Nothing else seems to explain what is going on here.

The Samaritan religion was rather complicated in those days, as was the Jewish religion. The Samaritans mixed into their religion pagan activities, much like what is happening in the church in America today.

The key to reaching people, from Jesus' perspective, was this Samaritan woman. He might not have reached the men of the community were it not for her.

Looking at this passage, you will find that as soon as Jesus touched on some personal issues, the woman turned the conversation to religion. "Where's the right place to worship?" In other words, "Who is right, the Jews or us?"

One thing hindering us in our ministry is that we get sidelined by insignificant questions. Everybody has a question, particularly when they feel backed into some kind of a spiritual corner.

This woman at the well believed in the Messiah and told Jesus that when the Messiah came, He would reveal everything to them. They were looking for the coming of the Messiah.

It is rather interesting that the religious leaders who knew so much about the law, which pointed to the Messiah, did not recognize Him when He showed up. That shows how important the law was as far as they were concerned.

Jesus said to her, "I that speak unto thee am he" (John 4:26).

It is hard to understand how this affected her—if she was beginning to feel that He was somebody who knew things that nobody else knew. Of course, He soon mentioned a couple of things that surely sparked her curiosity and gave her a sense of the contagious aspect of Christ's love. This was not something that could be explained to her, only experienced face-to-face with Jesus.

She could sense the passion in this man she had never met before who knew more about her than anybody should know.

She did not deny anything Jesus said, because she knew it was true.

Here was a woman who had a passionate heart. She made many bad choices throughout her life, as Jesus pointed out. He never condemned her for those choices but set before her a better choice.

The choices she made before this were based on the passion of the flesh. Now something different was stirring in her heart. The passion of the flesh gave way to something deep in her heart that she could not define.

Those who can explain everything happening to them are not experiencing the mysterious work of God in their life. The source of this mysterious working is the contagious love that Christ has. Let contagious love stir something within us as it did with this woman at the well.

Immediately this woman left her water pot behind, ran back into the city, and said to the men, "Come, see a man, which told me all things that ever I did: is not this the Christ?" (v. 29).

It was the contagious love of Christ that opened up to this Samaritan woman desires for God that she did not know how to tap into. Something in her heart responded to Christ, convincing her that this was the true Messiah.

She went back and got the men in the city and brought them all to Jesus. I would have liked to have seen that parade coming out of the city to Christ. Why did they follow her? What was it about her that convinced them to follow her?

They sensed something in her, some passion in her heart, and it stirred them to find out where in the world this had come from. They had never seen this in her before.

Not knowing what was happening, they were experiencing the passion of the flesh replaced by the contagious love of Christ.

Jesus spent a couple days with the Samaritans, and many of them came to believe in Him as the Messiah. The comment they made about this was most significant. They said to this woman, "Now we believe, not because of thy saying: for we have heard him ourselves, and know that this is indeed the Christ, the Saviour of the world" (v. 42).

How refreshing is that? How encouraged Jesus was to see the love that He had for them develop into a love in them for Him. That is what contagious love is all about.

I would have liked to have sat down with that woman and listened to her talk about the Jesus she met at the well. We do not know what her condition was when she met Jesus. We can only speculate. All the love affairs that failed certainly had an effect upon her life.

Keep in mind that Jesus knew her situation before He even met her. He knew what her life was all about. In looking at this story we need to understand that what God is doing in our lives today has nothing to do with our pasts. This is how Jesus approached the Samaritan woman.

He began with her past so that she would understand that He knew what she was really like. However, it was not her past that was important as far as Jesus was concerned. He loved her where she was that day.

Do we really understand this? In the Christian church today, we have become so judgmental. Somehow, we have forgotten what it means to be born again. We have forgotten that the past has nothing to do with our present if we allow Christ into our lives.

Even from the pulpit, we hammer and hammer away at a person's past. We condemn the past in such a way that people think we can change the past. You certainly cannot change the past. That is why it is called "the past." The contagious aspect of Christ's love is that it rises up above everything we have ever done and opens a new door.

I must point out that there is a double standard here. I have noted that some carnal rascals slip into the church without our Lord's approval. Maybe they are rich. Maybe they are great singers. Whatever it might be, we give them a free pass into the church.

We are busy denouncing that which God opened His arms to receive while permitting that which God hates. The Samaritan woman went and testified to the only people she knew and who would listen to her. The Lord knew that, but He had about Him the brightness of the revelation, and He understood the woman was completely sincere. It is hard to find someone who is completely sincere.

The Bible never gives us the name of this Samaritan woman. Even though she had a terrible past and in many regards was not a good woman, she responded to Jesus in a way that changed her life.

I am so thankful that Jesus did not put together some program to entice this woman to come His way. That is what we are doing today. We trick people into coming to church thinking we are doing the Lord's service. Jesus' encounter with this woman was not a well-oiled program from man's point of view.

Thinking about this does not encourage me, but how many people have been pushed away from Christ because of the program mentality of many churches today?

The Samaritan woman had emotions. I know we are a little leery about that word *emotion*. We say a man is very emotional when we mean he is very erratic, loses self-control, cries over nothing, laughs over nothing, gets blue over nothing, and gets delighted over nothing.

No, my brother and sister, that is not an emotion. That is a condition a man is in. He needs prayer and rest.

This may get me into trouble, but I believe we need to resurrect the phrase "religious affections" and demonstrate those affections to the cold, steel, deep-freeze Christians of the present day who only engage with text and theology and are afraid of emotions. Why don't we show them that religious affections and the spiritual emotions of the modern day are not the same thing?

The Samaritan woman had a collision. Her heart had a violent moment of contact with the heart of Christ, and the result was an experience the woman would never forget and, of course, the Lord never forgot. A stroke from God had fallen upon her and changed her life forever.

I am sure many religious things are done out of curiosity. But this woman's words stirred the men. From her time with the Savior, she carried a contagion. She had been deeply stirred and moved, and it showed when she raced into the presence of these men. Christ's love was contagious, and they caught it at once.

I suppose an element of religious adventure was there, but it was only an element. I think the main motivation for their getting up and hurrying to meet Him was that she had stirred them to the depths of their beings.

We need more of the religious affections that the Samaritan woman had in our churches today. But we calculate. We put together a "witnessing formula," thinking that if we do the right thing and say the right thing people will automatically become Christians.

Oh, but the love of Christ has such a contagious element to it that that never works.

Our testimony does not convert anybody. A testimony may only excite a person to get them going in the direction of God. That is the glory of the Christian witness. Christian witness never saved anybody, nor can it. It is the honest confession of what the Lord has done for me, and that may stir others to go and do likewise.

However, we must embrace that God loves to forgive big sins more than He does little sins because the bigger the sin, the more glory goes to God, who forgives. God not only forgives great sins but enjoys doing it, and as soon as He has forgiven them, He forgets the past and trusts you as if you had never sinned. God doesn't only forgive great sins as quickly as little sins, but once He has forgiven them, He never brings them up again.

Christ died for all, and anybody who will come will have their soul opened. With this woman at the well, somewhere in her soul a window was opened and the light of God finally shone down through it. God will use any witness to start, but no one can substitute for Jesus himself. The new life has to be born in us, and the new life will not be born until Christ and the sinner meet and through Christ the sinner defeats his will and comes out of the dust. He will always remember that encounter.

That kind of encounter, a meeting of the soul with God, comes with the freshness and the brightness of the new dawn. I believe we are where we are in religious services in

America because we have taken our religion secondhand. We are programmed by what we have been taught. We accept what people tell us; we do not push on to know Him so that we can say, "Now I know for myself."

God never intended that our hope for heaven should rest upon the words of a man, but power must come into our lives in the presence and the revelation of the knowledge of Christ, the Son of God.

6

Christ's Convicting Love

Heavenly Father, in the name of the Lord Jesus Christ Thine only Son, I praise Thee for the awesome conviction that Thou hast brought into my soul that led me to conversion. May I continue to seek Thee and find Thee each day. Amen.

> And a certain man was there, which had an infirmity thirty and eight years. When Jesus saw him lie, and knew that he had been now a long time in that case, he saith unto him, Wilt thou be made whole?
>
> —John 5:5–6

At the pool of Bethesda was a great multitude of people who needed healing, and all of them were waiting for the stirring of the water, including one man, we are told, who had lived with an infirmity for nearly forty years. When Jesus saw him, He knew the man's history and asked, "Wilt thou be made whole?"

The man answered, "Sir, I have no man, when the water is troubled, to put me into the pool: but while I am coming, another steppeth down before me" (John 5:7).

Jesus told him, "Rise, take up thy bed, and walk" (v. 8). Verse 9 says, "Immediately the man was made whole, and took up his bed, and walked."

When our Lord Jesus tells the man, "Rise, take up thy bed, and walk," it is to be understood as a command. But we should also see that what the Lord commanded here was impossible, according to the world. He not only commanded the impossible, He commanded the unimaginable, for this man could not get up, much less pick up his bedding.

After thirty-eight years, surely this man's muscles had atrophied and his body had stiffened into a kind of living rigor mortis. For a man to get up suddenly after all those years was unimaginable. Nobody there would ever have dreamed he could do it, including him.

We are living in the hour of big talking. But the man could not talk himself out of his condition. Today, many recommend we try this. If you will simply talk something up, you can do it, they say. Not only could the man not talk his way out of it, nobody else could do it for him.

Today, there is a new religion—what I call a Johnny-come-lately religion because it does not go back very far. It is based on the theory of the subconscious. There are a great many strange theories of Sigmund Freud, and this teaching is simply that human ills result from morbid memories and fears, mostly contracted in childhood, but they can be cured by being talked out. The idea is that if you will simply start talking, the well will begin to flow and pretty soon the poisonous juices somewhere within you that are causing your trouble will reach the surface and overflow and you'll be all right.

Unfortunately, this thinking has seeped into our churches so that now we are teaching pastors that if they can just get people to talk, people can talk themselves out of weakness. They can talk themselves out of foolishness. They can talk their way out of anything.

I would not say that confession and a certain unburdening of myself to another would not help. Do not the Scriptures tell us to confess our faults to one another? I believe when someone goes to another who is feeling blue and cheers him up a bit and shows him the silver lining, he may help him over the hump.

So some help can come from talking. It does not hurt to stick your chest out and say, "I can do it." It is a psychological lift, a good thing. But I believe that when talk becomes a religion, as it has in the day in which we live, it is nothing else than delusion leading men to death and hell. Because you cannot talk a weak man strong and you cannot talk a sinful man clean. You cannot talk a polluted man pure, and you cannot make the dead live by talking. All of the modern schools of religious talking never would have been able to help the man at the pool.

This is the reason I do not have many kind things to say about religious fellows who call themselves preachers and use the name of Christ when they drag in the theories of the subconscious and the theories of Sigmund Freud and the complexes and all the rest. They are no more prophets of God than the four hundred prophets of Baal who served under Jezebel.

Jesus could say an impossible, unimaginable thing—"Get up and take up"—to a paralyzed man because there was power in His words. There was no power in the man's words. There was no power in the words of those who lay around with him in their helplessness or even the people who passed by and tossed a grudging coin. There was no power anyplace there. The power lay in the words of Jesus.

A little later Jesus would say, "It is the spirit that quickeneth; the flesh profits nothing: the words that I speak unto you, they are spirit, and they are life" (John 6:63). God's almighty words are living words, and they are creative words. Take the very beginning, when God spoke into being all of creation. His words have the power of 10 million times 10 million atomic bombs.

But notice, there had to be a response on the part of the man who had been sick. This is really important. Immediately he was made whole and he took up his bed and walked. The ability to obey came with the decision to obey.

I know how dull that sounds, but if you get ahold of it, it might help you. Again, the ability to do the impossible came with the decision to obey God and try to do the impossible. Jesus said, "Get up and take up." There was power in those words to make the impossible possible and to bring to pass that which could never happen in the natural.

In the soul's encounter with God, there is what we might call a zone of darkness where the action is obscure and out of our hands. When the sovereign God steps in with His creative, life-bringing words and performs that secret and mysterious act that the soul cannot understand.

There is also a moment between being lost and being saved when the soul stands poised and the creative word has been spoken—"Get up and take up"—yet there is no power there. Faith has to do something wonderful. Faith has to make a leap across the gap and dare to do that unreasonable, super-rational thing and believe in Christ.

When conviction comes upon a person, the terror of God is upon his soul, and a sense of conscience and lostness and despair drives the soul into a corner. That is conviction, but it is something we do not have anymore.

Everybody is talking about the imperfection of present conversions. They say the conversions we do see are not radical enough, not extreme enough, and they can be explained. There is not much mystery, that sense of human defeat and divine triumph. There is not any of the despair that drives men and women to tears.

I believe I know why. It is because we have no conviction. We lack the sense of despair that Isaiah found and gave voice to when he said, "I am a man of unclean lips, and I dwell in the midst of a people of unclean lips" (Isaiah 6:5). Or what Peter felt when he said, "Depart from me; for I am a sinful man" (Luke 5:8).

We need today a visitation of awful, awe-inspiring conviction that will bring despair to the souls of men until they're driven into a corner and God Almighty drives them back into the darkness until they throw up their hands and say, "God, I'm a helpless and unclean man." Then in that hour, that strange, wonderful, mysterious thing will take place. The voice of Jesus will say to their hearts, "Get up and walk. Take thy bed." Strangely enough, they are able to do it. Strangely enough, the newborn can do it, and he does not know how.

Bluntly speaking, the supernatural element is not present in religion in our day. We get a little of it when we sing songs that stress it. But not always. I have been in meetings where the supernatural element simply was not there. There was no miraculous element. The soul was never driven into darkness to find itself sinking in despair and crying, "God, help me."

I want to see the Lord revive us again, but I don't want anything to do with these manufactured revivals that teach imitation. I want none of it. I would rather go under a tree somewhere and spend my Sundays there with a hymn book and the Bible than mingle with a cozy religion that makes Jesus Christ a great big pal.

7

Christ's Accountable Love

Praise Thee, O heavenly Father, for the Lord Jesus Christ who will be my final judge. May my life be in His care now and eternally. In Jesus' name, amen.

> For the Father judgeth no man, but hath com-
> mitted all judgment unto the Son: That all men
> should honour the Son, even as they honour the
> Father. He that honoureth not the Son honoureth
> not the Father which hath sent him.
>
> —John 5:22–23

Most people have a hard time dealing with the subject of accountability, especially in spiritual matters. We have the idea that anybody can do whatever they want and there will be no consequences.

As we come to understand Christ's love, we need to see that accountability is part of the picture. God has made us accountable to the Son. As John 5 says, "He that honoureth not the Son honoureth not the Father which hath sent him." This is important to understand. Many have a fuzzy idea of what love is all about. They have no idea that with Christ's love comes a sense of accountability. You cannot get away with anything as far as Christ is concerned.

As Christ pours His love into my life, He brings me to a point where I am answerable to Him. I am not answerable to some religion, some doctrine, or some celebrity preacher. I am answerable only to Christ. He is the one who has poured into my life His love, and I am answerable only to Him.

It is quite interesting to notice throughout the Scriptures that God does not give anybody a free pass. We like to do that, even in the church. Somebody does something wrong, and we give them a free pass because they are basically "good people."

Good people need to answer to God for every action they take. If we study the Scriptures, we will find out that when we stand before God, we will answer for every aspect of our life. The blood of Christ enables us to be cleansed to the point of receiving His love in its fullness. If we don't let the blood of Jesus cover everything, we will need to give an account before God.

We are prone to being intimidated by people around us who criticize us. Sometimes we fall for that trap and accept their criticism. But I am not answerable to people who criticize me; I am answerable only to God. That makes Christ's love an amazing aspect of my life.

By this, I do not mean that we should live an arrogant life with our nose in the air, ignoring the people around us. That is never appropriate. My final accountability is to God. If I am not honoring Christ in my life, I am not honoring God, and I will give an account to God for that.

Jesus gives many parables with a focus on the idea that when we come to Christ, we are stewards of whatever God gives us. We must recognize that we are stewards of this love and must understand this love and how it is affecting our lives. We need to allow this love of Christ to flow through us and touch the people around us. I am a steward of God's love in me, making sure it touches the lives of people around me. I will give an answer to God for that. This love that Christ has for me is not for my own personal consumption. Rather, it is for me to be a good steward and allow that love to touch the people who have yet to experience the love of Christ.

If we are going to have any influence on the people who are outside of Christ, it will only be because we are good stewards of the love of Christ within us. People need to encounter the love of Christ, and that can only come from people experiencing it in their own hearts and lives.

One aspect I enjoy thinking about is that Christ will give me as much of His love as I am willing to accept. That puts a lot of responsibility on me, but it also makes me understand that God will give me what I am willing to receive from Him.

And as I take that, it carries with it an obligation to be accountable.

If somebody loaned you $1 million, you would be accountable to that person for the million dollars. When God loans you His love from the Lord Jesus Christ, He will hold you completely accountable for that love when you stand before Him on the Last Day.

One thing that sometimes bothers me is that to some people, I will be the only Bible they will ever read, so to speak. Let me put it this way. To some people I will be the only expression of Christ's love that they will ever experience. That puts a lot of pressure on my everyday life, but God wants me to be in such a situation that I am not misrepresenting His love. I am not the creator of this love. I am only the channel through which His love touches people around me. Only in eternity will I ever understand the influence of God's love flowing through my life.

My life will be the only aspect of Christ and demonstration of His love some people will ever experience. Yes, I am going to be accountable to God. However, I am also accountable to the people around me to rightfully represent Christ's love. There is no other way these people will experience Christ's love.

I must make the point that I am now responsible and accountable to God to live the quality of life that He has provided me through this love.

I do not want to be the kind of person whom people feel sorry for, nor do I want to be the kind of person whom people ignore. I want to be the kind of person who shows the love of Christ in such a dynamic way that I will be creating in their hearts a thirst for God.

Thinking about Christ dying on the cross, I often question and say to myself, is the life I am living now worthy of the life that died on that cross? In my own strength, I cannot live up to that expectation. In my own strength, I could never be accountable to God for my life. That is why I need to open my heart to this love of Christ that brings into my life the solemn accountability recognized by God the Father.

My accountability as a Christian is not to the society around me. My accountability is not to the people around me. My accountability is not really to the church that I attend. My accountability is much higher than that.

I need to respect those around me and the brothers and sisters in the church, but I must understand that God is the one to whom I am at last accountable. He is the one who will have the final judgment of my life.

If I understand this, that everything I do or say will come before the judgment bar of God, I am going to walk very cautiously and I am going to walk in the power of the Holy Spirit.

To experience God's love is the only way I will be acceptable at the bar of judgment. As far as God is concerned, this love is not for my entertainment or enjoyment. This love has the serious effect of bringing my life into the accountability phase of walking with God.

When I do experience the outpouring of God's love and understand the dynamics of it in my life and through my life, I will experience no greater pleasure.

I like to read the Old Testament and see people like Abraham who walked with God. I often wonder what it really meant that they walked with God. It would have been nice to have been with Abraham as he was walking with God and to have simply experienced that fellowship.

I too must walk with God, and the only way I'm going to be able to walk with God is to have His love flow into my heart and life to bring me to the point of living a life that is worthy of Him.

Many times when we think of judgment, we think of the negative side. But there is also the positive side of it. As I walk with God in the power of His love, I will be rewarded for the things I allow Him to do through my life.

Many of today's Christians are fascinated by the idea of impressing God with the things they do. I must confess that I sometimes fall under that category. I want to impress God just as a little child wants to impress their parents with something they do, as if they could do something that their parents could never do. But I need to come to the point where my life is completely surrendered to God.

I think of that moment when Abraham laid his son Isaac on the altar. What brought him to that point, enabling him to do that? I honestly believe it was the outpouring of God's love. Abraham proved to God that his love for Him was stronger than his love for anything else in the world, even his son.

In Matthew 25:21, Jesus shares a parable concerning this idea of faithfulness. The master said to the servant, "Well done, thou good and faithful servant." I am so glad it does not say, "Well done, thou good and successful servant." Success seems to be our fascination. Faithfulness is the fascination of the Father.

With Abraham, his burning love for God overshadowed any aspect of success in his life. His love for God made him willing to give up everything.

If I am faithful in serving God on His terms, I put myself in the position where God's love can flow through me and touch the people around me. That is really what it is all about.

I believe that our great delight is to give back to God that which is worthy of Him. Not my works, but the love He has poured into my life.

I believe God desires the best, and I believe that I can give to God that best only because of the love of Jesus Christ in my heart.

8

Christ's Incarnate Love

O heavenly Father, how I praise Thee that even though I do not understand to the fullest the incarnation, I accepted Jesus as my Savior and I allow Him to guide and direct every step of my way every day. I pray this in Jesus' name, amen.

If I bear witness of myself, my witness is not true.
There is another that beareth witness of me; and
I know that the witness which he witnesseth of
me is true.

—John 5:31–32

When our Lord Jesus Christ came into the womb of the Virgin Mary, He came to share our grief and pain and bear our sins vicariously. For He himself never sinned. If He had, He could not have borne our sins, but He did.

The critics of vicarious atonement have much in their favor when they say that Jesus should not have died for us. It would be like a man brought up before a court of law and charged with murder and wrongly found guilty. The judge orders him to stand and then asks, "Do you have anything to say before sentence passes upon you?"

"Nothing, Your Honor," the innocent man replies.

The judge continues, "You have been found guilty after due process of law and after a fair and just trial. A jury of your peers unanimously decided that you committed premeditated murder, and the laws of the state under which you live require that you die. Therefore, I sentence you to hang by the neck until death."

You can imagine observers asking, "Another man commits the murder, and the judge here sentences this man to die in place of the guilty man? Where is there any justice in that?" It's this kind of thinking that makes critics throw the whole idea of vicarious atonement out the window. You cannot transfer moral responsibility from one person to another person, they say.

The strange part about it is, they are right. There never was a transfer of moral responsibility from one personality to another in atonement. Evangelists and preachers have taken theology and made complicated what was very simple.

When Jesus Christ was on that cross, we became part of Him and He became part of us, so that in one sense when He died we all died. Instead of the law putting one man to death for all, He put all men to death and raised from the dead all who believe in Jesus Christ so that every man dies for his sins. The sinner dies alone and the Christian dies in Christ. But every man dies for his sins.

Either he dies by joining his heart to Jesus Christ and the body of Christ or he dies alone in his sins. Recall the terrible words Jesus used, "Ye shall die in your sins" (John 8:24).

Christ, the head, gathered us all up into himself and died as we died. And because He was God, His death for us meant atonement and resurrection. If we had died alone and in ourselves, there would have been no resurrection unto eternal life.

But because we died in Him and with Him, there is a resurrection unto eternal life and the new birth and glory to come.

Jesus became man not by stepping down from deity into manhood, but by taking up manhood into God. The incarnation was not a degradation. God did not degrade himself. When Jesus Christ became man, He humbled himself but He did not degrade himself. The Deity never degraded himself and never will. When the holy Son of God walked among sinful men, there was no degradation.

If the whole church of Christ could get ahold of that idea and meditate on it prayerfully for just a day, it would lift Christianity infinitely beyond where it is now.

At the incarnation, Jesus became all that man is except sin, but in doing that, He took the man up into all that God is except deity. That is why He was among us. That is why we are theists, not deists. That is why we say there is a God, and He is the transcending God, high and lifted up, with His train filling the temple. Logic would say that He could not be among us, but the mystery of the incarnation says He could be and tells us why.

Isaiah said Jesus took our grief and our pain and our sins, took our future and our destiny, and carries them all in His heart and upon His shoulders and He didn't receive anything in return. He left the earth, but He did not leave humanity. He took them with him. Jesus is both God and man, and He is seated at the right hand of God.

He is the firstborn among many brethren. The little brother was lost, so the firstborn went to find him. The shepherd was there for his sheep.

Reason says to the shepherd, "Why are you out searching in the darkness? The night is settling in, and there are beasts out here. Your wife and children are waiting for you to come home. The kettle is on the stove, and supper is waiting. Why are you here?"

The shepherd's response? "Up the hollow, somewhere there's a sheep."

That is all the reason I need. All the logic I need. The shepherd came for the sheep. Where would the shepherd find the sheep except for where the sheep were? If the sheep could get to him, he would not have had to come, but because they could not come to him, he came to them. The wonder of the incarnation is more than a theological proposition. It is highly emotional.

Big brother came for the little brothers. The shepherd came for the sheep. God came for man. The Savior came for the lost, and He is still here. Though unseen by mortal eyes, He is with us every day. The mystery and wonder of His presence among us is that He came for us. The Son of Man came to seek and to save that which was lost. That is His explanation.

9

Christ's Silent Love

Heavenly Father, words cannot express the hunger and thirst I had within before Thee. May Thy Holy Spirit move within my heart in such a way that Thy love will shine through my life. In Jesus' name, amen.

When Jesus therefore perceived that they would come and take him by force, to make him a king, he departed again into a mountain himself alone.

—John 6:15

We live in a culture addicted to noise. If you live in a big city, you are certainly aware of how noisy life can be.

I can understand why Jesus in this passage goes up a mountain alone. He got tired of the noisy crowds. He had to go where He could be alone and just be with God.

I often think how wonderful it would have been to be there with Jesus on that mountain. To watch Him and see how He spent His time in silence before God.

It is quite natural for one to be noisy. When a child is born, all he or she does is make noise. We progress to a life of talking and talking and talking. However, there comes a time when we need to escape noise and embrace silence. And that is what Jesus is experiencing here.

When I think of Christ's silent love, I think of the fact that Christ does not always have to speak to us.

When somebody talks about love, love, love, it is probably because he has no idea what real love is all about. Likewise, when I hear preachers talking and talking and talking about some doctrine, I wonder if they really understand what it means.

If I have to tell someone I am a Christian, I am not living a life that pleases the Lord. I need to allow Christ's silent love to flow into my heart and life so the people around me can see there is a difference in me.

When we talk about people seeing Christ in us, it is not that they see Christ in us, but rather they see in us something they cannot explain. And of course, we know that to be Christ.

I must confess that many times I get so tired of the noise in the city that I do something that may seem strange in some people's eyes. I get on a train leaving Chicago and go west for approximately three hours. Then I take a return train for three hours back to Chicago. During those six hours, I am in one of those little rooms on that train by myself, nobody bothering me and nobody talking to me. And it is in those six hours when I am alone and silent before God that I begin to experience a fresh and a new sense of the silent love of God. God does not have to tell me He loves me. God's presence in my life reveals to me that which is the love of God.

To really experience the silent love of God, we must first empty ourselves of everything. That is a chore for us to do. We have grown accustomed to many things in our lives that we do not think we can live without. We become hoarders, in a way. But this silent love of Christ requires me to get rid of everything that would put distance between us and God.

When Jesus went up to the mountain, He left everything behind Him, even His beloved disciples, to be alone and spend time with the Lord.

I think the discipline of silence should be the focus in my life. If I am going to experience the silent love of Christ, I need to be silent myself.

Everyone has that relative who, whenever you are talking, talks over you, and there is no way that you can get a word in edgewise. I wonder if God the Father sometimes thinks that way about us. In our prayer life, we just chatter and chatter and chatter and chatter. We give God no time or opportunity to minister to us. We give Him our grocery list and expect Him to do everything that we ask Him to do while we go on our merry way.

What would it be like to be silent before the Lord and allow Him to do whatever He wants to do?

There are times when I'm alone in the church office that I get on the floor and prostrate myself before the Lord. I lie there and wait upon Him. Often, I do not know how long I stay there. I just know that I am before the Lord in silence. I do not interrupt that silence; I let this silent love of Christ flow into me.

I think so many Christians, especially pastors, are frustrated and discouraged because they are trying to do everything on a 24/7 basis. We do not give God time to silently minister to us through His love.

This is one reason why I am so drawn to some Christian mystics. They have a lot to say, including about how we need to get quiet before the Lord.

I have tried to do that all my Christian life, and the older I get in the Lord, the more important it is for me to be quiet before Him.

I remember when I was young I had a lot of things to say to the Lord. (I had more wisdom then than I do now, I think.) But as I get older and understand more about the Lord, I want to spend more time in silence before Him, just listening to what He has to say. Many times what God has to say cannot be conveyed with words. God moves in silence, which is very important for me in my Christian experience.

Out of the silence comes the work that God has for me.

I remember reading about Charles Finney, the great evangelist of a bygone generation. Sometimes when he preached he would get weary and exhausted. So he would cancel everything and go into the woods and stay before God in silence until the fire was restored in his heart. Then Finney would get up and go back, and the fire would spread through the congregations as he would preach.

I like that. I like a man who understands what it means to let God move in his heart and life.

I am not Charles Finney by a long shot. But I do understand the necessity of getting alone with God, away from everything else, and climbing that mountain or whatever it might be to spend time in quietness before the Lord.

When I think of Jesus and all of the people who flooded toward Him, I am sure it was a weary ministry to Him. Remember, He was a man while He was here on earth and experienced all of the limitations of man, including exhaustion. And I think it was in those moments when He went to the mountain alone in silence before God. I want to follow my Lord in that regard.

Yes, I am a preacher and a writer, and words are very important to me. But more important is coming in silence before the Lord, allowing Him to nurture my soul and spirit as He wants.

At that point, I do not give God any instructions. I just surrender myself before Him, close my mouth, and let my mind focus on the Lord Jesus Christ.

In our society we have many distractions. Sometimes we get all caught up in the culture around us—caught up in sports, politics, and even religion. All of this takes time away from our relationship with the Lord.

I think it was George Mueller who said that for every hour he preached, he would spend ten hours in prayer before the Lord. I may have the figures wrong, but it was something like that. What he was saying was, before he could preach he needed to spend time alone with God. And I believe that is true. As I experience the silent love of Christ in my life, I feel energy I cannot explain.

If you can explain everything in your life, you are not living for the Lord. But as I walk with Him in quietness, in silence, He nourishes aspects of my life that I do not even know are there. I have strength now, and it does not come from study. It does not come from exercise. It does not come from eating. It comes from silently waiting before the Lord.

In our 24/7 kind of society, we do not have much time to wait for anything. If we are a minute late we are in an uproar. So that is why I feel it is important for me to spend quality time alone with God.

I pray when I go to bed, but sometimes I am so sleepy that in the middle of my prayer I fall asleep. I need to get to a place where I can just lie before God and allow the quiet, silent love of Christ to nourish my ministry and my heart.

In our churches today, noise is a great attraction to so many people. The noisier the event, the more people will show up. I believe that is a trick of the enemy to keep us from the silent love of Christ.

How do we know when the Holy Spirit is really working in our hearts and lives? How do we know that it is the Holy Spirit and not enthusiasm?

We know it is not enthusiasm when we quietly wait upon the Lord, giving no instructions and simply submitting to a moment of time in His presence.

We all know what Jesus had before Him as He was ministering with His disciples: the cross. He needed many quiet times before His Father in preparation for that great eternal event.

We also have a cross we need to bear. And if we bear that cross, it is only because we have quietly waited for the silent love of God to strengthen us and give us the motivation.

Motivational speakers today want to work us up, get us excited about something. I suppose that's all right, but it is nothing I am interested in. I want my motivation to come from the silent love of Christ in my life. I want my ministry to be of such a nature that it is inexplicable to everyone, even myself. It is the silent love of Christ that motivates me to go forward on a path that I am not familiar with.

Many times we are so caught up in the valley that we cannot find a mountain to depart to where we can be alone with God. That sometimes is the enemy keeping us from the strength of our ministry. I refuse to allow the enemy to control my spiritual life. I refuse to allow anything associated with humanity or human strength or intellectual strength to determine my ministry for the Lord. Therefore, like Jesus, I will climb the mountain and spend time alone with God to experience the silent love of Jesus Christ.

10

Christ's Solitude Love

My gracious heavenly Father, I quiet my heart before Thee and seek the solitude necessary to hear Thy voice. Respond to me in a way that will glorify Thy name. In Jesus' name I pray, amen.

When Jesus therefore perceived that they would
come and take him by force, to make him a king,
he departed again into a mountain himself alone.

—John 6:15

I want to look again at this passage where Jesus departs
to the mountain alone. It is easy to establish from the
New Testament that this was a practice of our Lord
and nothing unusual. Our Lord every once in a while left
the multitudes and went by himself into a desert, up into a
mountain, or under the trees in the olive garden.

Jesus is not singular in this practice. Throughout the
Scriptures, you will find that the prophets also sought to be
alone with God. David's psalms are psalms of loneliness.
They are also psalms of sweet social joys, but those times of
social joys were interspersed with times when he and God
were alone.

Why did so many worthy people in the Bible withdraw from human society for periods ranging from a few hours to many days, waiting alone in the presence of God?

We live in a world with darkness all about us. Breaking the power of darkness is one of the great challenges we have as Christians. But the answer is not to completely retreat from society. We are to retire frequently from it.

Retire from human society and expose the darkness in your soul to the sunlight. Then the light of God will shine down on you and you will absorb God's ways, God's thoughts, God's emotions, God's personality. Then when you are thrust back into the darkness of society again, you will shine with the reflected light, a borrowed glow.

The saints always had their lonely times—times when it could be said of them, "himself alone." They were obeying God. They were alone not to retreat from reality but to retire from society and commune with God.

There is a reason Jesus went up into the mountain. People surrounded Him all day long. Their jealousy and their evil talk and sheer worldliness took a lot out of Him. He became tired. What was He going to do? Surrender to it all? No. He sent the multitudes away, and He went up into a mountain himself alone. He turned His troubled soul upward and for a long time exposed His soul to the face of God. And when those sweet and precious hours were over, He came down the mountain again. He came to still the waves and to bless mankind. Jesus could not help the multitudes by staying among them. He had to help them by retiring and getting power so that when He came among them He would have what they needed.

We must retire frequently from society to commune with God.

Moses, in the Old Testament, is a wonderful example of this. He studied all of the learning of Egypt, but when God wanted to use him to deliver the children of Israel, He had to give Moses another "degree"—one that took Moses forty years to earn in the backside of the desert. Oftentimes, the only sound he would hear would be the munching of the sheep as they ate in the darkness under the stars. God put Moses in school—the school of silence.

There Moses learned the therapeutic value of silence. God instructed him that he needed to get alone to learn it. All of us need to go to this school of silence.

When the strain of society got to be too much for our Lord's human heart to endure any longer, He sent the people away and He disappeared. They looked everywhere for Him but could not find Him. He was bathing His heart in silence.

What is sending men and women to premature graves with nervous breakdowns and heart failures? It is noise, tension, and pressure. Living in the middle of this world, we cannot escape from it, but we can retire from it sometimes. We can get alone, break the pressures, push away human society patiently, and quietly wait on God. You will learn more when you retire unto God than you would ever learn in all the Bible schools. You will learn more as you bathe your soul in silence and turn your face up to the light of God in retirement.

The question is, What is the purpose of retiring from society, into the secret silence, to wait on God and turn our hearts up toward His sunshine?

In my study and in various places, I have knelt with my Bible open and shut out every noise, locked my door, and waited. Soon you begin to have a sense—it is not an emotion at all. You are as calm as can be, and there is a sense of absolute well-being. A sense of complete harmony with the universe, a sense of being where God is—a refreshing, healing, delightful sense that can only come from being in tune with God and retiring from crushing society, allowing God to speak to your heart.

I could not quote what God says. And it is not anything you can see. It is far beyond that. It is deep, deep in the heart.

Jesus escaped the toils and the magnetic, strangling influences of society by retiring from it sometimes, warming himself at the heat of God's love and calming himself in the stillness.

We must do the same thing. The reason we are such shallow students today, backslide so easily, and get discouraged so thoroughly is because we live on the surface and in the noise.

What we hear today is that we must seek social integration and social adjustment. These ideas sound so learned that they must be right, but they are not. *Social integration*—now what does that mean?

Social integration simply means that we should submerge ourselves into society completely. But telling me to submerge myself in a society that has already lost, to lose myself in that lost society, is like telling me to chain myself to the deck of a sinking ship.

The other emphasis is social adjustment. Somebody experiences a bit of anxiety, and they see a psychiatrist, who tells them, "The trouble with you is you're not adjusted. Now sit down and let's talk this over. You've got to adapt and adjust to society."

The Bible does not teach adjustment and integration. It teaches repudiation and detachment.

The Christian is one who has been saved from a lost society. So when somebody says, "Get integrated back into that society," my response is, "Excuse me, but I shall not. I have a tough enough time seeking the face of God with tears. I had a tough enough time being converted and saved and renewed and regenerated, and I have a tough enough time keeping that very society from striking me down."

If I retire frequently to be alone with God, then, when I come back to society, I have something for it. I can help, because I have come down from the high place and have something to say. But if I surrender to them and let them beat me down and frighten me and intimidate me and absorb me, I will have nothing for them at all. I am just as bad as they are.

How can I bring truth to hopeless people when I have a hopeless heart beating in my bosom? How can I calm them when I am all excited myself?

The Lord tells us to go into the silence, and "when thou hast shut thy door, pray to thy Father which is in secret; and thy Father which seeth in secret shall reward thee openly" (Matthew 6:6). Then in calmness and assurance, we come down from the high place and into the dark valley where frightened people are running everywhere, trying to get integrated. Our message to them is, "You don't want cheap integration. Seek repudiation. Turn to God and say an everlasting yes, and with those same lips, utter an everlasting no to society." Detach from the harmless parts of society and repudiate the harmful ones, for there are some things in society that are not harmful.

Appreciate what is not harmful, but then turn your back on those things and raise your affections to heaven above, where Christ sits at the right hand of God. Never let anything in society master you. Detachment is the word.

As for harmful, evil parts of society, repudiate them. Say an everlasting no to all that is dark and evil and low, and when you do and you believe in Jesus Christ, your heart will be converted. You become born again, a new creature in Christ Jesus. Old things pass away and all things become new. But still, the magnetic power of society is all around, so while you live on the earth and follow the Savior, it will be necessary to retire frequently from society in order that you might break the stranglehold on your life. Destroy society's power over you, and when you come back to it, you come back as the master, not the slave.

Retire sometimes from the crush of the world, from all human society, including your family. Retire and shut your door, and there alone with God you will grow in grace. You will become calm while the world screams and rattles and blows its terrible whistles around you. When you have had your soul blessed, you can come back down where the poor, tired, noisy world is whistling past its graveyards and talk to them about something worthwhile.

You cannot be spiritual by learning a certain rule. You cannot be spiritual by taking a certain pill. You can only be spiritual by cultivating spirituality. I want to rearrange my schedule so that I can retire sometimes from the crushing society for a little time with God, cultivating spiritual things and calming my heart and listening to God speak in the silence. I do not say how frequently. I do not say how long. I just say that something like this has to be done if we are going to break the magnetic attachment of society upon our poor hearts.

11

Christ's Sovereign Love

Gracious heavenly Father, I praise Thee for that freedom which Thou hast given me, and I pray that day by day, not only would I respect Thy sovereignty but I would obey Thee in all things, regardless of how much it might hurt me. In Jesus' name, amen.

> No man can come to me, except the Father which
> hath sent me draw him: and I will raise him up
> at the last day.
>
> —John 6:44

I am a fundamentalist on the edges and an evangelical all the way through. But there are those who say that the Jehovah of the Old Testament became incarnated in the New Testament, which is false. It was not God the sovereign Father who became flesh and dwelt among us. It was Jesus Christ the Son who became flesh and dwelt among us. There is a distinction there.

Take, for example, Psalm 110, which starts with, "The Lord said unto my Lord." Who was David's Lord? Jesus. Who is it that sits at the right hand of the Father? Jesus.

It was the Son who became incarnate, not the sovereign Father Jehovah, the great I Am. Yet the Son was as much sovereign, as much *I Am*, as the Father. What can be postulated about the Father can be postulated about the Son.

What can be said about the Father and the Son can also be said about the Holy Spirit.

God is sovereign. He is free to always do as He pleases and fulfill all His good will without hindrance.

The primary will of God touches all of His eternal purposes. In His primary will, He does His will in heaven and earth and someday we will bow and declare that Jesus Christ is Lord to the glory of God's eternal purpose. That is why I can relax and not worry about the future. I am not scared, because I know it is going to work out all right. The secondary will of God is the will He has given people—a right to exercise that will, even when it opposes God.

God has a purpose for the universe, for the earth, for the human race, for the church, and for Israel. Moreover, every one of those has a specific, interlocking purpose, which God himself brought out of His own triune heart before the world was—when there was not a cloud in the sky, nor a drop of water in the ocean, nor a star in heaven nor an angel beside the throne.

The primary will of God is like a great ship. It pulls slowly and majestically away from the pier and starts toward the ocean. The ship's captain is responsible for getting that ship to her destination. That is the purpose. And the ship's owner, captain, and the crew are to carry out that purpose. In the meantime, a great many people on the ship do not know a thing about that purpose.

A little baby might be crawling around the deck, and a weary mother might be lying out there trying to get a little sun, and a little boy who can barely see over the side might be playing shuffleboard. Others might be playing cards and just naturally doing as they please. They are not paying any attention to the purpose of the captain. He knows what the purpose is.

His primary will is to get that ship to the final dock at last. The secondary will is that you can do as you please. As long as you are decent on board, the captain will not bother you.

Sometimes I hear people say that if God is God, why does He not stop all of the nonsense in our world? God knows where He is taking the ship, and all of His purposes will be worked out. In the meantime, His secondary will allows people to oppose His will, to be careless of His will, or to be ignorant of His will.

Imagine you are on board a ship and it is moving at so many knots, but you decide you want to get off the ship. You start in the prow, the front of the ship, and walk to the stern. You say to yourself, "I'm not going." But you will be going all right; do not think you won't be. The reality is, you would just be getting some exercise. Even if you determinedly walk in the opposite direction, the old ship would be carrying you forward.

Many people might be walking against the direction of the ship. But don't think for a second God will not have His way with them at last. It will be heaven or hell. Heaven for those who do His will and believe in His Son, and hell for those who do not. God is in charge of His great purpose, and while He allows people to have much freedom, He still fulfills His purpose.

The question that needs to be put forth is, If God is sovereign and has His will and cannot be hindered, how can men be free? I believe in both the freedom of man and the sovereignty of God.

God's sovereignty is His freedom to always have His way and to do His will. Man's freedom is his right to say no to

God's will and go in the other direction. How can you bring them together?

You bring them together like this. When God in His sovereign freedom created the heavens and the earth and all things that are therein, He made man on the earth, put a soul within him, and said, "Now to man I bequeath a limited freedom and the right to oppose me within limits. Use your own free will. I sovereignly declare that it is my will that you should have your will."

When man rises up against God, he is exercising the free will God sovereignly gave him. When Judas, for example, turned his back on God and sold the Son of God for thirty pieces of silver, he was fulfilling God's will just as much as he was using the freedom God gave him. Instead of canceling out the sovereignty of God, he was using the limited freedom God sovereignly had given him.

When I refuse to obey God, I am only doing what God has sovereignly given me the right to do. That's God's secondary will. That does not mean everybody is going to be saved. Those are to be saved who are repentant, believe in Jesus Christ, and are born again. Man in his freedom has the right to make his own choices on the little deck of that moving vessel. If he makes choices that are contrary to the will of God, it is because God says, "You're free to do it if you want to. I give you that freedom."

When a man raises his fist against God, he is not forfeiting the will of God. He is fulfilling God's gift to him, which made him free.

God deals with the men and women whom He has created as fallen creatures. He does this by testing them and teaching them and instructing them. They shall all be taught of God, Jesus said, and so He teaches, tests, and instructs them (John 6:45).

It is a great mistake to believe that every person who has heard the gospel has been evangelized. There are some people to whom God cannot talk. Having ears they hear not, and having stone hearts, they cannot obey. Many like to attend pleasant church events, but their souls are not open to God at all. They hear the Word, but they do not obey the Word. Rather than being taught by the Father, they are manipulated into believing in Christ and make such poor, hopeless Christians.

How is this different from the message some churches tell people of "Come when you want and do what you please"? This is a modern heresy and is not biblical. There is no place for it in the entire Scriptures, for "no man can come to me except the Father which hath sent me draw him" (John 6:44).

If God's people would only pray until the presence of God becomes as thick as the fog and then walk around with a sense of reverence and fear and repentance, the effect on others would be that their sin would become intolerable to them and the thought of death and hell's judgment would be unbearable. Converts would come bounding forward. Rather, we jockey them and prick them and massage them into the kingdom of God, and when they get in they do not know what it is all about.

12

Christ's Persistent Love

Thank Thee, heavenly Father, for pursuing me so persistently. I surrender my heart and life to Thee. May all I do please Thee through Jesus Christ my Lord. Amen.

From that time many of his disciples went back,
and walked no more with him.

—John 6:66

So why did these followers of Jesus leave Him?
Jesus himself was the reason. He boldly presented
the gospel, and for that reason many followers turned
away. Our Lord did not subscribe to the philosophies of our
day—that we are to trim or dilute the gospel to the expecta-
tions of the public in order to win them to Christ.

There are churches today that play catchy music and say,
"We hope this way we can win people to Christ." I ask, Who
converted whom there? Did the pastor convert the brethren
using red-hot music, or did they "convert" him? I suspect I
know which one was converted.

In the first two hundred years after Christ died, Christians
converted the Roman Empire as they were set on fire and
drowned and thrown to the lions and left to rot in prison

and beheaded. That was how Rome treated the Christians, and all the time Romans were being converted to Christ.

Then along came Constantine, and Christians no longer lost their heads, but they did lose their power. They conformed to the Roman world, but our Lord did not modify His doctrine.

People either took Him as He was or they did not take Him at all. Nobody apologized for what Jesus taught. Peter never went around saying that even though Jesus said, "He that eateth my flesh" (John 6:56), He really didn't mean it.

Many followers were drawn by His miracles. He was a gracious and wonderful man who talked to them about God, heaven, and other spiritual things. As their hearts warmed, their eyes surely misted over, and they thought, *Ah, this is good. We want to hear this.* But ultimately, they went back to their homes and wanted no more to do with Christ.

Why? Read John 6:26–27:

> Verily, verily, I say unto you, Ye seek me, not because ye saw the miracles, but because ye did eat of the loaves, and were filled. Labour not for the meat which perisheth, but for that meat which endureth unto everlasting life, which the Son of man shall give unto you: for him hath God the Father sealed.

People had come to the Lord and wanted to identify Him with economic success. This same thinking has become a modern-day heresy. We have married capitalism and Christianity and tried to make economic success proof that Jesus Christ is who He says He is.

People say things like, "I didn't have a dime before I trusted in Jesus Christ, and now ten years have passed and I'm enjoying economic success." I don't mean to be unkind, for I am, in a way, a Christian businessman myself. I preach for these brothers and sisters; I love them and count them as good friends. But the idea that if you become a Christian your profits will increase is hogwash. Nothing in the Bible teaches that. In fact, the Bible teaches exactly the opposite.

Christians in Jesus' time and in the book of Acts did not experience big success. They did not have wads of money. No, they lost everything for Christ's sake. And still, a bunch of carnal people wanted to identify Jesus with economic success. Jesus, however, cut through that idea, saying, in effect, "I know your crowd. You follow me because you think I have a restaurant and you can eat free for the rest of your life. You seek me not for spiritual reasons, but because you ate of the loaves and were filled. That's why you seek me."

The second reason followers turned away from Jesus is found in John 6:28–29:

> Then they said unto him, What shall we do, that we might work the works of God? Jesus answered and said unto them, This is the work of God, that ye believe on him whom he hath sent.

Jesus made their eternal hope to depend not upon their labor, but upon their right relationship with himself, whom God sent. That was a big shock. Still today, much that is religion is simply a moral laboring for eternal life. People are doing this, doing that, laboring, putting down this, and putting down that. They are doing good things. But they leave undone what the Lord talked about in verse 29. Before anything else, they need to develop a right relationship with Christ.

The sinner jumps up and says, "All right, God, I'm at your service. I have a wonderful voice, and my IQ is way up there among the treetops. I have a good education; I have degrees and a lot of other stuff." Basically, they say, "If you have me, Lord, you've got something now."

God's reply? "I do not need you, and I do not want your works. I do not need your activity."

Salvation does not come from doing; it comes from a right relationship with Him whom He has sent. Believe on Him who has sent Him.

Another reason people in Bible times and today leave God is found in John 6:30:

> They said therefore unto him, What sign shewest thou then, that we may see, and believe thee? what dost thou work?

They wanted a sign.

We have this type of people among us today. If you cannot do a miracle or two, they will not believe you are a child of God. Their attitude back then was, "If you're what you claim to be, show us a sign. Our fathers had their signs; you give us a sign."

Jesus flatly refused.

Here is what a certain group within the church forgets. They forget there is such a thing as moral truth. There is such a thing as miraculous truth too.

Our Lord Jesus did and still does miraculous things, but not to prove anything. The Lord will heal a man if He wants him to live. He will raise a baby up from their cradle of death, but not because some old deacon is demanding He do it. Jesus would not do it for the devil's sake in the desert when

He had been in the wilderness for forty days and nights, where He flatly refused three times to perform a miracle.

John the Baptist did no miracles, but he was a conscientious, moral voice in the wilderness. I am not speaking against miracles. I happen to be among those who believe the days of miracles are not passed. I believe that if we have faith and the need is there and is spiritual and not carnal, the Lord our God will answer prayer and do wonders for us even today. I believe that if we were the kind of people we ought to be, we would see more of the Lord's wonders in the land of the living. I have sense enough to know that the Lord himself is the only sign that is ever going to be given to His believing people.

He came, He bled, He died, He rose, and that is the moral proof of God. And when the Holy Ghost came from heaven like a silent flash of light entering the breasts of men and women, nobody could ever argue again about Jesus being the Christ. They rose from their spots and preached that He was the Christ. He was His own proof, and He is His own proof today. The holiest sign this world could ever have is a man who lives rightly in a bad world; a woman who keeps clean in a dirty world; a young person in high school who keeps her heart and mind and body clean in a dirty school. There is your miracle. There is your sign. There is your wonder. There is your proof.

Holiness is its own proof; righteousness is its own sign. Nobody yet has been able to invent an excuse or an explanation for righteousness.

People want Christianity. They particularly want the gospel to be a kind of beanbag that can be tossed around and grabbed by anybody so that they can hide it or hold it and do as they please. Jesus took it out of their hands and essentially said, "I am the sovereign God, and I am in charge, and my Father is in charge," and He gave it to the morally prepared person.

Jesus taught them that there was a moral preparation. Not to deceive the good but to save the bad—people who know how bad they are. This is moral preparation. The Lord did not come to save the righteous; He came to save the sinners who knew they were sinners. When a man knows he is a sinner and knows how bad he is and has his heart opened by the voice of God, he still is lost, but he is prepared to be saved.

The flippant, the insincere, the superficial, and the shallow make religion a jukebox. Put a dime in, press a button, and get this jukebox religion.

Jesus took it out of the hands of dying men and said, in effect, "God Almighty moves among man, and by His Holy Spirit He's reaching and finding the prepared ones." The ones who have heard and listened and know how bad they really are. That is moral preparation leading to repentance. Hearing that, His followers went back to their homes.

I know there are hundreds of people who go back to their same lives from hearing the gospel.

Then we have John 6:53–58. The crowds wanted religion that they could get their hands on to label it, cut it to measure, and wear it. But the Lord said, to paraphrase Him, "You'll never get salvation that way. You either get salvation through me or not at all."

The truth of God stands. We ought to believe it as it is, and if we do not, we will perish. In Jesus' day they said, "We won't take that kind of stuff."

If your service to the Lord Jesus Christ depends upon "wearing" religion, you are not serving Him rightly. You are not serving God until you can serve Him without anything to eat. "The flesh profiteth nothing" (v. 63). A man who thinks he cannot serve God without a tailored coat and shirt is not serving God—He is serving the flesh.

The amazing quality of God's love for all of us is that He is always persistent and never changes. What brings me to Christ is that which keeps me in Christ.

13

Christ's Loyal Love

O Father, there have been times that my loyalty to Jesus has been challenged. My weakness did not get me through, but Thy grace and faithfulness keep me on the path of loyalty to Thee. In Jesus' name, amen.

> Then said Jesus unto the twelve, Will ye also go away? Then Simon Peter answered him, Lord, to whom shall we go? thou hast the words of eternal life. And we believe and are sure that thou art that Christ, the Son of the living God.
>
> —John 6:67–69

While Jesus was on earth, He inspired many people to follow Him. He created such a stir that just about everybody was talking about Him. You could say He was a celebrity.

But as we read the Gospels, we see many of His followers slowly retreat. Perhaps they wondered if it was worthwhile to follow Jesus. Maybe they thought they were wasting their time.

Many churchgoing people have done that in recent times. They still keep up their church membership, pay their tithes, and even give to missions. Nevertheless, they have allowed themselves to get to a state where they are not truly following the Lord anymore. Their hearts are not really in it. They just have not turned away with their feet yet.

As we discussed in the previous chapter, John 6:66 says, "Many of his disciples went back," which are terrible words to read. I suppose that not one of them ever stopped and considered what they were returning to.

His disciples had lived with Jesus and surely had come to feel the warmth of His loyal love like the sun in springtime. They had looked into His eyes and certainly felt something going into their hearts when they did. They had heard our Lord quietly and sweetly preach to them. His friends had walked with Him and stood beside Him and called Him by His first name or, respectfully, Master, the name given to a teacher. Yet when they became aware of the cost of following Jesus fully, many decided to withdraw from Him. What were they going back to?

Let me suggest a few things I think they were going back to.

First, they were going back to their sins. As 2 Peter 2:22 tells us, they went back to their sin as a dog "is turned to his own vomit again; and the sow that was washed to her wallowing in the mire."

Second, they went back to their loneliness and hunger. After you have once walked with Jesus, even briefly, you can never be anything but lonely if you withdraw from Him. Without Jesus, we also miss out on the bread of life, for "he that cometh to me shall never hunger" (John 6:35).

Third, they went back to their fears, for Jesus takes away our fears. But now, without our Lord, they would again face their fears and remorse.

Before we decide to turn back from following Jesus Christ, we had better find out what our lives would be like. I will say it plainly: There is not one desirable thing about living without Jesus.

After seeing many of His disciples turn away, Jesus turned to His beloved twelve and asked, "Will ye also go away?"

I suppose that the human Jesus, in one panicked, awful moment, wondered if the last disciple would leave Him and He would stand alone as a failure. Here was Jesus' heartbreak—His cross before the cross. And yet there would be other "crosses" to bear, including when Peter denied his Lord and when Judas sold his Lord and the disciples forsook Him and fled.

Still, I like what Peter said. "Lord, to whom shall we go?"

At first I wondered if that was impulsive, blind loyalty on Peter's part. After considering this reverently and prayerfully, I do not believe Peter's response was like that of loyal fans of some politician who know he is losing but still keep feeding him optimism and hope until the last ballot is counted. I do not believe this was loyal Peter trying to heal the wounds of Jesus and comfort His heart before they drove Him to Calvary. I very much doubt that.

I think Peter had been tempted to turn away from Christ, but when the others went away, it was likely the culmination of long days of discussion over what Jesus had said and what kind of life He had been living and what kinds of demands He'd been making upon them. Peter, of course, had heard the gossip, and maybe he even took part in it. Peter probably considered whether he had been right to leave his father's fishing boat and follow this wonderful, strange figure who walked up and down the hills and plains of Galilee and Judea. Peter undoubtedly searched his own soul, but thank God he decided that there was no place to go, no one to *whom* he could go. Note that he did not use the impersonal "what"; he used the personal: "To whom shall we go?"

Peter had walked with Jesus until a "whom" had formed in his mind, not a "what," not a religion, not a creed. Again, he did not say "To *what* shall we go?" but "To *whom* shall we go?" A Person had begun to move into Peter's life. The others left to a "what."

Now, where shall we go and to whom shall we go if not Jesus? Back then, some might have said, "I will go back to a more ornate religion." I do not know if this was the case, but the simplicity of Jesus surely was a stumbling block. There was something dramatic when men with long beards and long robes stood on street corners and made long prayers. It was dramatic, too, when they mounted the steps of the temple, singing, and when the priest offered sacrifices. Something about it all appealed to the flesh in a major way.

Into this world came a quiet man who said people should worship Him in spirit and in truth and that external religion is like a tomb filled with a dead man's bones (Matthew 23:27). He made other statements like, "Unless you eat the flesh of the Son of God and drink his blood, you have no life in you" (my paraphrase of John 6:53) and "Out of the hearts of men comes evil" (my paraphrase of Matthew 15:19). Perhaps people were disappointed or confused by these strange statements and wanted to go back to an external, ornate religion.

I would never waste my time with that kind of religion.

If you insist upon having everything done up fashionably, you do not have far to go to find a church that will satisfy you perfectly. If you want ornate religion, the world is full of these types of churches. They can spend thousands of dollars on extra flourishes, but when it is all over, they do not wake up one slumbering man or woman from their grave. Ornate religion cannot cleanse a person's heart from lonely sin. It cannot take away one bit of remorse or remove the shadow of death from a person's mind. It cannot purify his soul or cleanse his spirit. Yet there are those who insist that religion has to be ornate. The simplicity of the gospel church is the simplicity of Jesus and no one else.

There are churches that will let you do practically anything but commit murder and still be a member in good standing. There are churches where you will never be embarrassed. The Word will be taught so sweetly, the preacher will purr over you like a tabby cat, and it will all be so lovely and sweet. There are churches like that, and I recommend that if you don't want to go to heaven or follow the Lamb, if you don't want to bear the cross, it's all right to go to that kind of church. It is not possible to be a true Christian and never know the reproach of Christ's enemies. Never have anybody sneer at you, call you old-fashioned, and wonder why you are like that. But you can be a church member now and never know the cross, never have an enemy, never have a narrow way and never get a thorn in your foot, never feel the cross in your heart, never suffer, never walk into danger, and never lose anything. There are churches like this that will never even ask you if you have been converted.

For some today, the demands of Christ are too exacting and the thorns too sharp. Many want it easier with an easier church and easier religion. If you go back, think what you are going back to. Back to sin, to distress, heavyheartedness, darkness, the grave, and judgment.

14

Christ's Assuring Love

Thank Thee, O Father, for the assurance that I can have in Jesus Christ. Although all the world is against me, I find confidence and comfort in the bosom of the Lord Jesus Christ. In His precious name I pray, amen.

Then Jesus said unto them, My time is not yet
come: but your time is alway ready. The world
cannot hate you; but me it hateth, because I testify of it, that the works thereof are evil.

—John 7:6–7

Here we see how perfectly poised and self-assured our
Lord was in God His Father. He was perfectly free and
uninfluenced by public opinion. He was not forced to
be reckless in keeping up His reputation.

It is wonderful to be free and poised and self-assured
like that. To be free to say "amen" whether anybody else
is saying it or not. To keep perfectly quiet when everybody
else is excited and to stand still when everybody else is
running.

Most of the time we go along with the crowd, particularly
our brothers and sisters in Christ, but Jesus our Lord was
not stampeded by the opinions of the people.

They said, "Why don't you go to Judea?" Jesus replied, "I'm not going to Judea. I'm staying in Galilee." (See John 7:3, 8.)

He might have been concerned that someone would call Him a coward. If He had gone to Judea, though, He would have been under bondage to that person who was accusing Him of cowardice and gone to Judea outside of the will of God. However, Jesus was sure of himself in God, so He stayed in Galilee.

When everybody is doing a certain thing and you see it is not right for you, obey your conviction. Too often we let ourselves get jockeyed into doing things God doesn't want us to do. We care too much about what people will say.

Jesus did not care what the people said. He stayed in Galilee because He did not want to put himself in jeopardy before the proper time. Our Lord would not walk into a trap; He would not go into an ambush there in Judea. He knew people would say He was just afraid, but He was so completely free in God that He let them think and say what they wanted.

Let us remind ourselves that our Lord Jesus Christ did not know fear. He stood against King Herod and called him "that fox," because He was not afraid. And when the time came, Jesus went up to Jerusalem.

He told the people, "I'm going up to Jerusalem, and I'm going to fall into the hands of the Jews. They will sell me to the Gentiles, who will crucify me, and in three days I will be in the earth" (see Matthew 20:18–19). He was not afraid of them. He walked up boldly and did what He had to do in the will of God. He was neither afraid to be thought a coward nor was He a coward. He was right in God's eyes.

That is a good lesson I wish we would learn. Many times one of the Lord's people will do things under bondage to other people's consciences because they think his testimony is not quite consistent. A man ought to be free to say to God, "God, you will lead me," and then say to possible detractors, "God is leading me, and He does not expect me to do what you expect."

This was exactly what Jesus did. He stood before Pilate without panic. He had had His blood-sweat in the garden of Gethsemane. He poised himself, was sure of himself and unaffected by the consciences of other people or public opinion, and went calmly out to die. He would not even be turned aside by the kind but badly directed sympathies of His people. He did what He did, and that was that. That's the number one lesson for us today: God's people must get out from under bondage to each other.

In Jesus' day, the people were creating Jesus in their own image. They said, "Depart hence, and go into Judea, that thy disciples also may see the works that thou doest. For there is no man that doeth anything in secret, and he himself seeketh to be known openly. If thou do these things, shew thyself to the world" (John 7:3–4).

They could not understand this selfless man. They did not know how to appraise the man who did not have an ax to grind, or anything to gain, for that matter. Our Lord was here to die for people, not to win them to His political side or even His religious side. He was here to die for them and save them.

Jesus faced real cynicism. The word *cynic* comes from the Greek word for *dog*. The cynic today is a philosopher who believes with the devil that every man has his price. The old

Greek hedonistic philosophy says everybody moves for his own ends, and everything we do is for our own ends.

This hedonism and cynicism has lasted through the years. It was criticized by great philosophers, but it has been in human nature all these years.

Someone once said that when a man put money in the cup of a poor man on the street corner, he did not put it in the cup in order to help the poor man, but to make himself feel good. Now that is cynicism. That is the devil's doctrine, the doctrine that every man has his price.

There are two things we can learn from all of this. First, be careful about judging other people's motives. You never quite know why a man does a thing. You might think you know, but you likely do not, particularly if you are not in sympathy with what he is doing. So let us not judge each other's motives before the proper time.

The second thing is that your own family may be the last people to accept you. That is one of the hardest things for us to grasp. Why is it that our own family is the last to believe in us? Jesus' own brothers, born of His own mother, did not believe in Him. His brothers were not His disciples. They grew up with Jesus, played together with Him, and saw Him grow. Yet they said, "Why, we know this boy. He's our brother. What does He know, anyhow? We know as much as He does." They were right from a human perspective, but in reality they were wrong because they did not accept Him as Lord. I suppose it was hard for Jesus—the human Christ—to take that His own brothers did not believe in Him. Still, He told them, "The world cannot hate you; but me it hateth" (John 7:7).

Why did He say this? Because they were part and parcel of the world, and a house divided against itself cannot stand.

The world's people can quarrel and bloody each other's noses, but basically they are one spirit. That is why it is so hard to make people see that the spirit living in the unregenerate world is anti-Christ and anti-God. Throughout his epistles, the apostle Paul tells us plainly the same thing: The spirit that dwells in the world is hostile to God and to Christ.

This thing many people call a peaceful coexistence between the born again and unbelievers is a myth. They that are born of the flesh persecute those born of the Spirit even today.

A peaceful coexistence can only be maintained by unworthy compromise on the part of the people of God. Christ is altogether of another Spirit. The two spirits are entirely hostile. I do not understand why people do not get this. It is so simple and biblical.

It is found in the writings of the saints and is part of the theology of the church of Christ. It is the traditional evangelical belief of the saints from Pentecost to the present hour, and yet today people do not see it. I always feel that I'm out of gear with my times when I remind people what's plainly taught in the Scriptures—that the Spirit indwells the born again and the world is anti-God and anti-Christ, hostile to God and not subject to the law of God and unable to be subject to it.

When we become truly born again, something is born into us that is hostile to the world. Not hostile to the poor, suffering, and dying people of the world, but hostile to the religion of Cain that fills the world.

He that is born of the flesh persecutes him that is born of the spirit. Our Lord, when He came into the crowd, made the heart condemn itself. Whatever makes the heart condemn itself will never be forgiven by the one condemned. Keep that in mind.

You can talk religion to people and they will come back for more, but when you are so Spirit-filled and so in touch with God that your life, demeanor, and very presence are pure and Christlike, it rebukes the sinner and makes his own heart turn against him and condemn itself. He is a marked man and will not be forgiven until conviction comes on his soul and he falls down before his God and finds hope.

Our conviction must be that we will have no part in meetings that simply console the saints, give them more assurance, pat their carnality, and soothe their carnal backs. When we take a stand against sin, we are going to raise the anger of those whose hearts feel condemned because of our stance.

Today, they have given us the right to be a religion, and it is quite the proper thing to say something nice about God. But it is one thing to say something nice about God and quite another thing to be so in God that your very breath makes the hearts of men condemn themselves. They will not forgive you for that.

You can talk all you want about religion being good for mankind, and people will approve. You can say, "I think there ought to be churches in every community," and people will nod and say, "That's right." You can say, "I believe that the teachings, the morality, upon which America was founded ought to be restored." We all would nod and say, "That's right. That's good."

But when you get past that Cain religion, the religion of patriotism and shallow philosophy, and get to the point where it is either Christ or damnation, you will not be liked.

You're going to find that same spirit rising up against you because the Spirit of Christ and the spirit in the religious world are hostile to one another.

Not everything that does good is good, and not everyone who is capable of doing good sometimes is to be trusted. That is the great divide.

Jesus Christ cannot be tolerated as being merely good. He must be either obeyed or rejected; one or the other. But this is the day of the tolerance of the Lord Jesus. We are tolerating Him now in the civilized world. He gets into newspapers and magazines. His name is used over the radio, songs are sung about Him, and speeches are made. He is the tolerated Savior.

No, no, a thousand times no; He cannot be. I am not a prophet, but I think a little common sense will help us to see something.

We are a scared people now. People are talking about turning to God and being religious. We are comfortable with saying He's a good man. But we are not making Jesus Christ Lord of our lives in this country, and we are not drawing the line and saying, "I believe in Him not as a good man but as my God and Savior and Lord."

I believe religion ought to be promoted. I think we ought to do better and acknowledge the Lord, and when we say we are one nation, indivisible, under God, I think we ought to emphasize that phrase "under God."

However, it needs to be more than "in God we trust." It needs to mean more than "under God." It needs to be more than friendly gestures in the direction of God. Before God Almighty's great power comes into a human life to make it over, there has to be an acknowledgment of the lordship of

Jesus. He is the Lord to the glory of God the Father, and we make that assertion now.

Jesus said, "He that is not with me is against me" (Matthew 12:30), and there can be no neutrality. To be for Him is to believe in Him, obey Him, and let the world know. There can be no underground Christianity.

15

Christ's Knowledgeable Love

Heavenly Father, I desire with all my heart to know Thee, but not just on the outside. I want to dive into Thy heart and know the depths of Thy love for me. In the wonderful name of Jesus I pray, amen.

Jesus answered them, and said, My doctrine is not mine, but his that sent me. If any man will do his will, he shall know of the doctrine, whether it be of God, or whether I speak of myself.

—John 7:16–17

It is easy to see from the New Testament that our Lord never attended any of the Jewish schools of His day. To many people around Him, He seemed to be just a common person, and that is why they challenged His teachings. How could someone uneducated explain what truth really is?

Back then, people believed knowledge came from the Pharisees, who studied the Scriptures for a long time. Truth only came through study. That is why they could not understand where Jesus was coming from. He did not fit their idea of a knowledgeable person.

Perhaps that is where we are today in the Christian church. We think that if a person has studied the Bible, he must certainly know the truth, and who are we to question him. That is our most fundamental problem today. Truth is not the assimilation of facts.

We fail to realize that every cult is based on some form of truth. And when the truth comes from people simply studying facts associated with the Bible, those people can always come to the wrong conclusion.

If I have a physical problem, I want my doctor to examine me, not go into his library, read some book, and then come and tell me what the book says.

Theology has been reduced to this sort of thing today. It is an assimilation of facts backed up by verses of Scripture from someone with a half dozen degrees after his name. There is a great possibility that what these people are teaching concerning truth is not really what God is trying to say to us.

This is what Jesus encountered in His day, and perhaps it is why He said, "My doctrine is not mine, but his that sent me" (John 7:16). Jesus did not come to modify or reinvent the truth. He came bearing the truth from God. And until we get to the point of understanding that truth is from God alone, we will never really understand what the Bible is all about.

I have said this many times, and I really believe it: All of the Bible is necessary to make it the Word of God. I can quote a verse from here or there and make the Bible say anything I want it to say, but it will not be God's truth.

God's truth does not come through a person. That was the problem with the Pharisees back in Jesus' day. They were taught what to teach from generation to generation. Along the way there was a little bit of twisting until what they thought was truth was a shadow of the real thing.

The people in Jesus' day had a very inadequate view of God's truth. It was the responsibility of Jesus to point this out and to correct their view of the truth. Truth is not something manufactured by a person, but rather it has to do with revelation.

From my point of view, the dividing line today is between what I call evangelical rationalists and evangelical mystics.

The evangelical rationalist says that the truth is in the Word, and if you want to know the truth, go to a scholar. The problem comes when a person does not see the supernatural, mysterious aspect of what this truth is all about. This kind of thinking will kill the truth of Christianity just as quickly as any liberalism will, and it'll do it in a more subtle and deadly way. Just because you believe something does not mean you have experienced it in your heart.

We are being told today that all you need to do is believe that Jesus is your Savior. I would like to challenge two aspects of that idea.

The first has to do with believing the truth. It does not take much for someone to believe what sounds true. If the right person says the right words at the right time, it is possible for anyone to believe anything.

The second aspect—the mystical level of knowing God— rises above the intellect and has to do with experiencing the truth. What good is truth if it has no transforming element in my life? To embrace the truth is to embrace God himself. Every truth is rooted in God, so in order to accept and experience truth I must experience God in my life.

The Pharisees were very good at twisting words. They could take a word and make it mean anything they wanted. The average person could not figure it out because they had surrendered to the fact that a Pharisee was a well-educated person, and therefore if anybody should know the truth, it was him.

Today, as I said, if a preacher has a half dozen degrees after his name, people will believe what he has to say, because, after all, if anybody should know the truth, it is someone who has studied the truth for many years. But again, it is possible to study the Bible for a long time and not truly understand the truth as presented by the Holy Spirit in the Word of God.

Because of this, in Jesus' day, people did not recognize Jesus as the Messiah. They were looking for someone quite different, someone who the Pharisees had manufactured in their own minds.

Could this be true of us today? Could it be that men and women are twisting and manufacturing who Jesus Christ really is? How many people have been tricked into becoming Christians and have not really been born again?

This is a serious issue. We cannot teach words—we must teach the truth, and Jesus said, "I am the way, the truth, and the life: no man cometh unto the Father, but by me" (John 14:6).

These are not just words that we nod our heads to and say, "I believe that." Rather, it is truth, and the truth is Jesus Christ. I am not embracing a theology. I am embracing the person of the Lord Jesus Christ.

The reason so many Christians today are struggling with their Christian life is that they have not crossed the threshold of being born again. They have embraced the truth and doctrine. They agree they must be born again and want to be born again. But somewhere along the line, they have been duped into believing something without actually experiencing it.

We are being taught to trust the body of truth but have forgotten that truth has a soul. That is why I believe we must fill our minds with Scripture, but it must not stop there. Get as much Scripture into your heart as possible, but there is another step absolutely essential to your knowledge of God. That is when the Holy Spirit comes down and takes possession of your soul.

We must have Bible teaching. We must know what the Bible says. We must have the body of truth, because the Holy Spirit will never come into a vacuum. And as we prepare our hearts and souls for the Holy Spirit to come, He comes in a way that transforms us into the likeness of Christ.

This experience is probably the hardest experience someone will ever go through. Becoming a Christian is not a convenience. It involves spiritual warfare. The enemy does not want anybody to know the truth. The enemy does not want anybody to embrace the knowledge of the Lord Jesus Christ as their Savior. He will do anything and use anybody to keep us away from that.

This brings me to the subject of discipleship. I am all for discipleship, and I believe that every believer needs to be discipled in his or her Christian walk. But we have turned discipleship into an educational experience. We see discipleship as simply learning about Jesus and keeping His commandments.

Maybe that is why we are in such a rut today. We can know the truth, but if we have not experienced the truth, we do not have any viable knowledge of God.

As we yield ourselves completely to the knowledge of God, we begin to experience this God. I do not want to just know about God. That may be okay for religious people, but I want to know God with the fiery enthusiasm of men like

Paul. Nothing could come between him and embracing the truth of God.

Paul was a Pharisee, as you well know. But when he encountered the truth of God, he became a disciple of Christ. It cost him a lot, but from Paul's point of view, it was well worth it. He did not want to have a dead religion burdening him day after day. He wanted to be set free to worship the God whom he had come to love through Jesus Christ.

The sad fact today is that many going to our Christian churches are under the bondage of religion. They can quote a couple verses of Scripture. They pray during the prayer time at church. They give their tithe every Sunday. But if you talked to some of them privately, you would discover an emptiness in their life.

They are afraid to admit this to anybody. They want people to believe that they know the truth, when in actuality, all they know are phrases and words that have in no way changed their lives.

When Christ comes into my life, He brings the knowledge of the Father. Not something put together to make me feel good.

I must be honest and say that there are many things in the Bible that do not make me feel good. Sometimes in prayer, I am overwhelmed by a sense of conviction. I thought I had dealt with an issue, but in the presence of God, I realize I had merely expressed words. There have been times I have had to confess to God and wait for Him to flood my heart with a sense of forgiveness.

People talk and preach about forgiveness. Yet I wonder how many have really experienced the forgiveness of God. It is one thing to have knowledge about forgiveness, but it is quite another thing to experience that forgiveness in your own heart.

What Jesus says in John 7:17 is very important: "If any man will do his will, he shall know of the doctrine, whether it be of God, or whether I speak of myself." What person would ever say that to his audience?

Jesus is saying here that in order for us to really know doctrine we must be doing the will of God. When I am surrendered to God and His will, there will come flooding into my soul knowledge that is not of man but rather of God. I will know this because God has revealed himself to me in an unquestionable fashion.

16

Christ's Amazing Love

Dear Father of my Lord and Savior Jesus Christ, how amazing is my relationship to Thee. I rest not on yesterday and look not toward tomorrow, but I rest in the amazing aspect of Thy presence today. In Jesus' name, amen.

Then said Jesus to those Jews which believed on
him, If ye continue in my word, then are ye my
disciples indeed; And ye shall know the truth,
and the truth shall make you free.

—John 8:31–32

When Jesus said, "If you will come to me, I will
make you free," He insulted some people. "How
can you say you can make us free?" they asked.
"We've never been in bondage to anyone" (see John 8:33).
Jesus went on to explain that as sinners, they were servants
of sin, but I am afraid these people had lost their humility
and thus their power to learn. How could Jesus teach them
anything?

As soon as we think we know all the answers, we, too,
lose the power to learn. Ever try explaining something to a
person who always cuts in with, "Sure, I know that"? Pretty
soon you give up.

In Jesus' day, not only did some followers lose their power to learn, but they forfeited their hope because they lost their sense of personal sin. This would be their great woe. They did not say, "Wait a minute, this man says I'm not free. I had better examine myself." They said instead, "I know I'm free, and if He says I'm not, He insults me." Then they walked away angry, because Jesus had challenged them and said He could set them free if they became His disciples.

Humble followers who know they are sinners rarely get into this condition. It's a religious man who gets himself into this kind of fix. Religion is the greatest thing in the world, but it is also the most dangerous, because people can get entrenched in their beliefs concerning themselves. If they feel beyond criticism, there is not much you can do.

When we get to a point where we feel touchy being questioned about our spiritual lives, we have arrived at a state of death. We ought to keep very meek and lowly about our faith. If someone challenges my claim of being a Christian, instead of insulting me it ought to drive me to examine my foundations and see if the things in me are indeed true.

In Jesus' day, you could not get the religious to examine their own lives. They were completely untouchable and beyond criticism. And any upstart who suggested the entrenched religionists were not right was insulting them.

This is also a deadly snare for denominations today who claim to have a corner on the truth. People measure themselves against themselves and listen to the sweet music of their own self-praise until they believe they are better than anybody else.

Many Jews in Jesus' day were sure they were right and better than other people. If anybody challenged them, they pointed to the outward signs of their religion: the hills of Zion, the robes of the priest, the towers and well-worn steps of the temple, and their hundreds of years of history.

The same thing can go on in any denomination.

To protect themselves against the challenges of Jesus, the Jewish leaders ignored the fact that their own Scriptures described their four hundred years of bondage to the Egyptians. They forgot that in Judges 6:1 it says they were delivered into the hands of the Midianites for seven years. And Judges 13:1 states they were delivered into the hands of the Philistines for forty years. Their history of bondage goes on and on.

In Jesus' time, Israel was an occupied country under the domination of the Roman Empire. Yet these religious leaders dared to stand up and say, "We've never been in bondage to any man," deliberately trying to twist His words into a political meaning that they knew our Lord had never had in mind.

What these poor religious leaders did not know is, you cannot inherit spirituality. Even today, many will say, "My father was a child of God, so everything is all right with me." They do not know that the grace of God is given individually; it is not received by inheritance.

Someone once said, "[Moody] started a Bible College which has turned out many excellent men, but it has never produced another Moody."*

You do not become spiritual by going to a spiritual church and having it rub off on you. You become spiritual by going the way Christ's disciples did, by paying the price they paid,

---

*"Training for Missionary Work," *Precious Seed* 1, no. 11 (1947), https://www
.preciousseed.org/article_detail.cfm?articleID=3551.

by believing what they believed, and by sacrificing as they did, trusting and yielding and surrendering.

Jesus said to the religious leaders of His day, "You're not children of Abraham because you don't act like Abraham. Abraham was a friend of God, and I come from God the Father and still you reject me. How then can you be true sons of Abraham? You're acting like the sons of the devil and you're claiming to be the sons of God." And of course they got angrier and angrier. (See John 8:39, 44.)

I have been preaching a long time, and I want God to keep after me. I want Him to keep me penitent and distrusting of myself, so I never feel entrenched and unassailable. I will not allow yesterday's victories to tie me down and make me believe that I am a better man than I am. I want God's sun to rise in me every morning, expose the blemishes, and save me from entrenched privilege.

I believe we ought to examine ourselves. For example, what did your conduct prove you to be yesterday and last night and last week and last month and last year? You are the descendant of somebody, the son or daughter of somebody, and from somewhere you received your nature. What did your conduct prove your nature to be?

I believe that is a fair question. Are you the son or daughter of ambition, of desire, of evil thoughts, of evil words? Or are you a son or daughter of faith and love and compassion and humility and penitence? You can know that not everything is all right between you and God, but it will not be the sharp, proud knowledge of the Pharisees. Rather, it will be the meek knowledge of the saints.

You might say here that it is faith that saves us, not conduct. I agree fully. But conduct flows from faith just as a stream flows from a fountain. And if the stream from the fountain is dirty, the fountain is dirty too. You can know whether your life is flowing from a pure fountain by looking at your conduct.

Look yourself over. Look at yesterday and the day before. Does your examination tell you that you are acting in keeping with your holy character as a child of God? If it does, good. Thank God and be happy. But if it does not, that ought to disturb you.

You might ask yourself, "Wait a minute, how is it possible that I've been living by false premises? I thought I had been leaning on things that are sound."

It is one thing to know the truth. But the thing that changes lives is experiencing the truth. That is the amazing aspect of Christ's love for you and me. He enables us to experience the truth, which is himself.

Live humbly and meekly. As long as we keep alive in our bosoms a sense of personal sin, there is hope for us.

17

Christ's Extreme Love

Dear Father of my Lord Jesus Christ, Thy love for me is so extreme and beyond my full comprehension that it amazes me. I don't deserve Thy love, but I wrap my heart around that love and glorify Thee each day. Amen.

Then answered the Jews, and said unto him, Say we not well that thou art a Samaritan, and hast a devil? Jesus answered, I have not a devil; but I honour my Father, and ye do dishonour me.

—John 8:48–49

Are there limits to Christ's love for us? What happens if someone rejects the Lord? Is that the unpardonable sin we hear about?

Only one person in the Bible ever talked about an unforgivable sin, and it was Christ himself: "Wherefore I say unto you, All manner of sin and blasphemy shall be forgiven unto men: but the blasphemy against the Holy Ghost shall not be forgiven unto men" (Matthew 12:31).

There is our explanation. We read in John 8 that people attributed Christ's power to the devil and not the Holy Spirit; they were blaspheming the Spirit and committing the unpardonable sin.

You can reject the Son of God and still be pardoned after accepting Jesus. Rarely do people come to Christ the first time the Holy Spirit tries to win them over. They often resist, sometimes for years. If rejecting Jesus is the unpardonable sin, then their sins would never be forgiven.

Again, Matthew 12:31 says, "All manner of sin and blasphemy shall be forgiven," so speaking against the Son is pardonable but speaking against the Spirit is not. Why is that?

God the Father and His Son are external to us. Therefore, outside forces—the flesh, fear, ignorance, bad instruction—can lead a person to speak against God or Christ. But the Holy Spirit is the distilled essence of the Godhead; He is not external. He communicates himself inwardly past reason and teaching to our moral perception, our conscience, our human spirit. It is the profoundly mystical element in Christianity.

The people who dishonored Jesus were considered good people. They were the seed of Abraham, among the very best of Israel. They were Pharisees, scribes, rabbis—people who lived moral lives—but theirs was an external righteousness. They did not know the mysterious Spirit or God at all. Their spirits had rotted to the point of no return, where they could not know good from evil. Oh, they knew that things like stealing and adultery were wrong. But a spirit of evil lay within them.

Jesus fought against the false teachings of these scribes and Pharisees while He was on earth. He said they were like whitewashed tombs, "which indeed appear beautiful outward, but are within full of dead men's bones, and of all uncleanness" (Matthew 23:27). At other times He called them liars, false teachers, and sons of the devil because they were fully convinced of their own purity and wholly unaware of their sinful condition.

Today, there are people in our churches who will go to hell because they won't admit that they are wrong. They just do not want to lose face. They do not want to admit their condition. They believe in total depravity but think it has touched everybody but them. They might say, "I was born in sin and conceived in iniquity, and my righteous deeds are like filthy rags," but they do not believe it. They are lying to their own souls. Charge a person like this with doing something wrong, and see what he will do. He will turn red and curse you out.

It is right to admit you are a sinner. Inability to feel spiritual distress is a mark of a terrible condition. I do not say it is proof of the unpardonable sin, but I do say it is a proof that we are on our way to that. I cannot say too often that if you can be sorry for sin, thank God. Some people just cannot.

Jesus told a parable of two men who went into the temple to pray. One stood and prayed for himself, "Oh, God, I thank Thee I'm not like other men." The other man bowed his head and said, "God, have mercy on me, a sinner." I think the Lord smiled and said, "That's the way I like to hear him talk." And that man returned to his house justified. (See Luke 18:10–14.)

Years ago, the Lord impressed upon me the following passage:

For thy Maker is thine husband; the LORD of hosts is his name; and thy Redeemer the Holy One of Israel; The God of the whole earth shall he be called. For the LORD hath called thee as a woman forsaken and grieved in spirit, and a wife of youth, when thou wast refused, saith thy God. For a small moment have I forsaken thee; but with great mercies will I gather thee. In a little wrath I hid my face from thee for a moment; but with everlasting kindness will I have mercy on thee, saith the LORD thy Redeemer. For this is as the waters of Noah unto me: for as I have sworn that the waters of Noah should no more go over the earth; so have I sworn that I would not be wroth with thee, nor rebuke thee.

Isaiah 54:5–9

I have taken that last sentence, verse 9, as being completely for me, almost as if it had not been written for anybody else. God promises never to get angry with me again, which worries me a bit. The other day in my study I was telling God, "Father, this is terrible. Suppose I do things I should not?" In my heart I heard, "I know how to handle my children. I'll take care of that. I'll discipline you. I'll chastise you. I'll make you sweat. I'll bring you around. I'll see to it you don't get away with anything, but I'll never be angry with you or rebuke you while the world stands."

So I took off the old coat called Tozer and put on the robe of righteousness, Christ's righteousness. I am not worried about myself, because I know I belong in hell. The man who knows he belongs in hell cannot go there, because that is a penitent man, and a penitent soul cannot perish.

18

Christ's Faithful Love

Dear Father in heaven, I praise Thee that my relationship with Thee is not based upon my knowledge, which is so imperfect. It is based upon my faith in Jesus Christ, who has saved me from my sins. In Jesus' precious name, amen.

> I must work the works of him that sent me, while it is day: the night cometh, when no man can work. As long as I am in the world, I am the light of the world.
>
> —John 9:4–5

I do not preach psychology; I preach the Word of God. Yet I do think there is such a thing as the psychology of defeatism. When you are in a defeated state long enough you tend to want to stay there. An old dog who knows only his doghouse might venture out for a while, but he soon crawls back in. In many regards, we are like that. We are stuck in a rut.

In John 9, we read about a man who had been blind from birth. Sitting and begging each day, he surely had learned to live with his blindness and did not expect any other way of life. Human nature being what it is, he was probably in a rut and never thought he would see. But from somewhere there came to him the mystery of faith.

Now, everybody has faith in something or someone. But that kind of faith is mutual trust, not the faith that saves. The faith that saves is the mystery of God imparted to the human soul by the Holy Ghost.

When Jesus and His disciples saw the blind man, the disciples asked Jesus if his condition was the result of the man's or his parents' sin. Jesus said, "Neither hath this man sinned, nor his parents: but that the works of God should be made manifest in him" (v. 3). Jesus continued, "I must work the works of him that sent me. . . . When he had thus spoken, he spat on the ground, and made clay of the spittle, and he anointed the eyes of the blind man with the clay, and said unto him, Go, wash in the pool of Siloam, (which is by interpretation, Sent.) He went his way therefore, and washed, and came seeing" (vv. 4, 6–7).

That was a test of obedience. In other words, Jesus was telling the man, "I will give you faith enough to do what I tell you to do."

This blind man knew very little about Jesus, but he acted on the little he knew and was delivered. It is good to know the truth, but the idea that you have to know a lot in order to meet Jesus through saving grace is not true.

Before he was healed, the blind man had stared straight ahead, but now he looked around, seeing. He was the same man, yet so much was different. So it is with the sinner.

When a man or woman comes to the Lord Jesus Christ, repents of their sin, and trusts Christ as their Savior, something happens within them, something wonderful beyond words. They are the same person, and yet they are marvelously different. It causes neighbors to ask, "Isn't that the fellow we used to know and hang around with in the bars?" Someone else might say, "It looks like him, but what's he doing with the Bible under his arm? He cannot be the same fellow. He just looks like him."

If you have been renewed by the mystery of the Holy Spirit within you through faith in the love of Christ, you are in many ways the same person. God starts with the same stock, but oh, what a change. The old things are passed away, and all things become new.

As a young Christian, I was not satisfied just to be a simple fundamentalist. I wanted to be a bright fundamentalist and understand the arguments against Christianity, so I read more books on atheism and evolution than I did on religion. However, I knew God, and I wore out several Scofield Bibles to get my theology.

The arguments in those books did not throw me, because I had met God. I do not worry about atheists, unbelievers, and all the rest, because they do not and cannot know enough to disturb the foundations of my faith.

When the Pharisees challenged the blind man's faith in Jesus, he answered, "Whether he be a sinner or no, I know not: one thing I know, that, whereas I was blind, now I see" (v. 25). This is the final test of conversion, a personal experience.

Our problem today is that everybody has to have their thinking and praying done for them. If people can find a fellow who prays all night, they'll chase him all over North America and brush up against him in the hopes that some of the glory will brush off.

Do your own praying, do your own worrying, do your own trusting. Get down on your knees and seek God. Read your own Bible and suffer your own persecutions. Let the Lord lead you, and you will come out all right.

I believe there are three classes of spiritual blindness in the world.

First, there are spiritually blind people who know they are blind yet want to see. Jesus said He came to this world so that the blind would see (John 9:39). If we know we are inwardly dark and blind, we only have to cry to the Light of the World and Jesus will deliver us.

Then there is the second class: the blind who think they see. There are spiritually blind people who perhaps are morally accountable, but they do not see Jesus correctly. They look at things cross-eyed.

In this day of soft Christianity, we forget that the Word of God both kills and makes liars. We have forgotten that the same message that saves one person damns another. Two men hear it, and one will be saved and the other will perish.

I hold out hope for any person who will admit they are blind. In their blindness they have given way to temper, they have been jealous. They might have been stingy and squeezed a nickel until the buffalo bawled in pain. They may have been so nasty that only the mercy of God kept their spouse from leaving them years ago.

You may have been and done all of that, and if you say, "I'm not blind," you condemn yourself to everlasting night. However, if you say, "I'm too bad ever to believe, too bad to be helped," that is when God comes in for the rescue.

Hell is for the proud and the self-righteous, but there is a fountain filled with the blood of Jesus for the meek and the humble who come as they are without one plea and believe in Jesus Christ.

This brings us to the third class of spiritually blind people: those who were once blind but now can see. The light of the world is Jesus, and if you let Him shine in on your heart as you believe in Him, your darkness will turn to light. He will take away your blind eyes and give you seeing eyes.

19

Christ's Personal Love

*Dear heavenly Father, how I thank Thee
for that Shepherd who has come into my life
to personally guide me every step of the way.
I pledge to trust Him and His leadership in
my life. In Jesus' name, amen.*

I am the good shepherd: the good shepherd giveth
his life for the sheep.

—John 10:11

The shepherd and his sheep is a lovely picture of Christ
and His followers. It certainly is one of the most popular and best understood analogies in the Bible, even
among those of us not familiar with raising sheep.

In biblical times, the relationship of the shepherd to his
sheep was personal. Today's sheepherder does not know his
sheep this way. He might stand on a knoll somewhere, over-
looking his great flock of sheep, but he sees them only as an
undulating white surface. He knows the sheep are his; he
knows their size and how much profit they will bring him.
But he does not know them personally. To him sheepherding
is simply a commercial proposition.

This was not so with David. He didn't have many sheep,
but he knew them all personally. In turn, they stayed by their
shepherd, confident in his affection and protection.

As for today's sheepherder, his sheep have no confidence in him. They do not even know he exists. If he came into the herd and yelled at them, they would all run. The ancient shepherd knew his sheep from the time they were born. When they went astray, he caught them and carried them back on his shoulders. It was a warm, personal relationship.

That is the beauty of Christianity. It is faith that brings us into a personal relationship with the Lord Jesus Christ. As the old hymn by Eliza Hewitt says, "My faith has found a resting place, not in device nor creed."

If we believed in something but did not know who said it, nor where it came from or how it came to be, we would have a cold, heartless, mechanical religion. The person who turns from unbelief to this kind of religion is exchanging a chain of iron for a chain of gold, but it is a chain nevertheless, and it binds him as surely as the chain of iron bound him.

However, the man who has Jesus Christ lays aside all chains and is not bound at all. It is a personal religion—belief in the person of Jesus Christ our Lord. The person and the presence; these two wonderful truths make the Christian life what it really is.

⟪⟪⟪◯⟫⟫⟫

John 10:3–4 says the shepherd calls his sheep, and "the sheep follow him: for they know his voice."

Nobody likes to get up once they've bedded down, and sheep are no different. They like to rest and stay in the fold. So when the shepherd leads his sheep out, you know they are leaving a comfortable place. It is not until the shepherd's voice rouses them that they get up and go. The Scripture says, he "leadeth them out" (v. 3).

What was God's formula for the evangelization of the world? Following Christ's resurrection, He instructed the eleven disciples, "Go ye into all the world, and preach the gospel to every creature" (Mark 16:15). Later, when His followers were all assembled in Jerusalem, the Lord said, "But ye shall receive power, after that the Holy Ghost is come upon you: and ye shall be witnesses unto me both in Jerusalem, and in all Judaea, and in Samaria, and unto the uttermost part of the earth" (Acts 1:8).

But the disciples stayed in Jerusalem, and most were essentially bedded down until the Lord sent along persecution and drove them everywhere to preach the Word. The Lord led them forth, but He actually had to send persecution to get them out of their snug beds and going where they should go.

The Lord leads sheep out for a number of reasons. First, there is no food in the fold. The shepherd has to get the sheep up on their feet and lead them out to the green pastures that they may eat their fill and then lie down beside still waters.

Then, the sheep need to have some exercise. Sheep that lie down in green pastures and beside still waters are likely to get very fat and useless. Therefore, the Lord leads them out in order that they may get their exercise.

There is also growth and experience. Sheep that stay in the fold have no experience at all. Christians also must go forth. They must go forth to work, to travel, and to get experience. Jesus says with His analogy, "I lead forth my sheep." He did not say we were to be planted like trees in the yard.

I do not believe in isolated, insulated Christianity. I do not believe that sanctification is by insulation. I do not believe that God will make us holy by keeping us in a thick coating of moral and social insulation so we never bump elbows with anybody who does not believe exactly as we do. How do you know what you will do until you are put in a situation? How do you know what you will do out yonder if you never go out yonder?

Therefore, the Lord leads us forth so that we may get experience.

Being full of the Holy Ghost, Jesus was led into the wilderness to be tempted by the devil. The same Lord says that as He is in the world, so are we in the world (1 John 4:17). He takes us out of our snug places and into the world not to mingle with its pleasures. We are to be there as a protest and a conscience to the world. We as Christians have to meet our enemies. They are out there, but I want you to know that Christ is always before you.

Now, I do not know what your tomorrow will bring. No one does. It is better to be in the dark and trust God day by day than to know the details of what's to come. That is why I do not ever recommend that any Christian go to a fortune-teller or a seer or any of the rest. I do not want to know my future. One step is enough for me.

You may be coming into a critical period in your life. Some crisis may be only a few days or weeks or months away, and if you knew it were there, you would have weeks or months to worry. If you don't know what's coming, you have your Lord and will get through it all right. I do not want to know my tomorrows, and I do not want you to know your tomorrows. Only remember one thing: Christ is always there first.

Christ is not sitting back like a general in a comfortable tent, telling His soldiers to charge up to the mouths of the cannons. Where Christ sends us, He's there before us and

He's there with us. "Lo, I am with you always," He promised (Matthew 28:20). Remember, He will never ask you to go where He will not go. He will never ask you to do what He has not done. And He will not ask you to suffer what He has not suffered.

Our shepherd is always present. The most significant thing about the Christian life is that we are all sheep gathered around the Shepherd, and that Shepherd is actually in our midst. I believe His real presence is in the fellowship and hearts of His people.

A church that is focused on its pastor is a religious group, but a group gathered in the personal presence of Christ is the real church. How He can be among us and yet be at the right hand of God the Father Almighty is the mystery of the Godhead that I will never understand.

The shepherd could have sent word to the sheep and said, "Hold the fort, for I'm coming." The sheep would have fled in terror into the wilderness and probably been eaten by the lions. He did not say, "I'll be there after a while." Instead, He said, "I'm there now." As David, an earthly shepherd, attested, "Thou art with me; thy rod and thy staff they comfort me. . . . Surely goodness and mercy shall follow me all the days of my life" (Psalm 23:4, 6).

20

Christ's Sacrificial Love

Heavenly Father, knowing the Good Shepherd and how much He loves me and desires good to come to me, I want to praise Thee. I can trust Him to lead me and guide me in the way that will honor and bless Thee. In Jesus' name, I pray, amen.

But he that is an hireling, and not the shepherd, whose own the sheep are not, seeth the wolf coming, and leaveth the sheep, and fleeth: and the wolf catcheth them, and scattereth the sheep.

—John 10:12

This is not a pleasant topic, but it is an important one. In John 10:10, Jesus warns of a thief that "cometh not, but for to steal, and to kill, and to destroy." When the thief sneaks into the sheepfold, his purpose is to destroy the flock. Not only is he an enemy of the sheep, the thief is also an enemy to the shepherd.

Jesus presents here a picture of a religious racketeer, a person who enters the fold not to help the sheep but to fleece them. He may smile and pray and quote Scripture, but deep down he is cynical and depraved, a man who won't hesitate to use sacred things to be popular and make money. Some "healing men" will even hire people to come to a service and pretend they are sick. After these men pray for them, the people claim they have been healed and praise the Lord. There are other thieves in our fold who have discovered that they can prey on people's tenderness for foreign missions, and God's good, innocent, generous people will shell out their money.

In Ezekiel 34:2, the Lord warns the prophet to speak out against shepherds who feed themselves and not their flocks. Later in the chapter, God essentially says, "I'll fix them and send out true shepherds who will round up my flock and bless them."

Scripture also warns us about hirelings, who don't own the sheep they oversee. John 10:12 says that when the hired man sees a wolf coming, he flees.

Now, who is the hireling? He certainly is not as depraved as the thief, because he does not come into the sanctuary and pretend to be anything. He does not deceive; he is not a racketeer. He does not deliberately destroy like the thief. He is just a hired man. He generally puts in an honest day's work, but he has no personal interest in the sheep. He does what he does for a living.

This is the Christian leader who is simply doing what he does because he sees it as rather easy living. There is no love for the Great Shepherd.

Then there is the wolf. Satan is that wolf, of course, and the thief and the hireling are friends of the wolf, whether they realize it or not. After the thief and the hireling have caused or allowed the sheep to scatter, the wolf finds it very easy to go in and get himself a nice piece of mutton. As long as the sheep are gathered around their shepherd, sure of themselves, poised and careful, they are safe. However, as soon as they go wild and start to run in all directions, all the wolf has to do is just wait until one passes by, and then he pounces.

When the hireling sees the wolf coming, he says to himself, "I am working here, but I do not see why I should take a risk and face the fangs of a wolf." Then he disappears. They are not his sheep, he is not attached to them, they do not know his voice, and he does not know their names.

That is a terrible and ghastly description. But remember, these are not my words. Jesus put it in Scripture (John 10:12), and now we see that ecclesiastical history is replete with these sorts of things. Why? Because it is a fallen world and we are bad people and we need God. That is why. It is what might be expected in a bad world like this.

Then, there is the contrast: the Good Shepherd. Jesus said, "I am the good shepherd" (v. 11).

Jesus came down to earth and was incarnated to be the Good Shepherd, one who did not care for himself at all. He never performed a miracle for himself. His miracles were always for somebody else. He never asked anybody for anything for himself, except when He asked the woman at the well for a drink of water (John 4:7). And even then, He made the request in order to draw her into a conversation so He might win her to himself, which He did.

Again, what a contrast: thieves and hirelings and wolves against the Good Shepherd of the sheep. How we ought to love the Lord Jesus Christ. How precious He ought to be to us.

This shepherd proved that He loved us even unto death. What more can you do for anybody than to die for them? Yes, you can help them, which is well and good, but it may not inconvenience you. You can give them a good deal, but it may not be at your own loss. You can sacrifice something for them, but you will still have something left. But when you give your life for them, you do not have anything left. Jesus our Lord gave His life for His flock. He did not have anything left. That is a good shepherd.

⟪⟪⟪◯⟫⟫⟫

I want to address another picture in John 10: "Other sheep I have, which are not of this fold: them also I must bring, and they shall hear my voice; and there shall be one fold, and one shepherd" (v. 16).

Jesus has other sheep besides Israel.

Today, in some evangelical churches, as soon as you talk about "other sheep," they say, "Why don't you deal with the heathen at home?" And, of course, they never do anything about it. They believe other sheep exist and need to be saved in theory, but in practice they forget the other sheep.

The Word of God tells us that God has other sheep. They are lovely sheep; they are His sheep. There will be a day when they all will be in one fold, but now they are scattered.

The imperative here is in Jesus' words "them also I must bring." Not "I want" or "I hope to bring them," but "I *must* bring them." And He does this by sending found sheep to find His lost sheep. This must be the imperative of Christian missions. When He goes after sheep, He goes after them through His undershepherds.

21

A Closing Prayer

O Lord, we love Thee. We want to be restrained and conservative, but we want Thee to know and we want the world to know that we love Thee for loving us. We love Thee for coming for us. We love Thee because Thy holiness was not soiled and Thy character was not degraded when Thou didst come down to us. We love Thee for this, Lord Jesus, we bless Thee, we worship Thee, and truly, we can sing that Thou art the one in whose presence our soul does delight.

Lord, Thou art with Thy sheep, and Thou art searching them out in the ravines and gullies and between sharp points of rock and among the briars. Finding them here and finding them there, but finding them.

O Lord, we pray for any lost sheep today. We pray, Lord Jesus, that Thou wilt find that sheep. May that sheep no longer be in peril of its life. May it bleat until the Shepherd notices and comes, takes it on His shoulder, and carries it home rejoicing.

Blessed be Thy glorious name. We thank Thee for Thy great flock, for all tongues and tribes and nations everywhere, O Lord, that have been found. We think often of the lost ones, and we thank Thee for the found ones, who, like the sands on the seashore, nobody can number. Blessed be Thy name.

O Lord, too often we are more concerned that everything is all right with us. We are more concerned that we stand well in religion, that we have a reputation among the saints.

We thank Thee, Lord Jesus, that Thou sayest to such poor world wanderers as we are, "If any man will come after me, let him deny himself, and take up his cross, and follow me," and "Ye shall know the truth, and the truth shall make you free," and "If the Son therefore shall make you free, ye shall be free indeed," and "I am the light of the world: he that followeth me shall not walk in darkness, but shall have the light of life."

Thank Thee, Lord, that as we walk in the light as Thou art in the light, we have fellowship with Thee and with one another, and the blood of Jesus Christ Thy Son cleanses us from all sin. This is a greater treasure than all the gold and all the diamonds the earth holds.

Now we trust that Thou wilt send us out into the world under your quiet, sure gaze, and may we meekly disclaim all self-righteousness, humbly deny ourselves, and willingly take up the cross, sorry for all that is imperfect and wrong, glad for the blood that cleanses, and grateful for the grace that pardons and remembers sin no more forever.

Blessed be Thy name. Amen.

A. W. Tozer (1897–1963) was a self-taught theologian, pastor, and writer whose powerful words continue to grip the intellect and stir the soul of today's believer. He authored more than forty books. *The Pursuit of God* and *The Knowledge of the Holy* are considered modern devotional classics. Get Tozer information and quotes at www.twitter.com/TozerAW.

Reverend James L. Snyder is an award-winning author whose writings have appeared in more than eighty periodicals and fifteen books. He is recognized as an authority on the life and ministry of A. W. Tozer. His first book, *The Life of A. W. Tozer: In Pursuit of God*, won the Reader's Choice Award by *Christianity Today* in 1992. Because of his thorough knowledge of Tozer, James was given the rights from the A. W. Tozer estate to produce new books derived from over four hundred never-before-published audiotapes. James and his wife live in Ocala, Florida. Learn more at www.james snyderministries.com.

More Resources by A.W. Tozer and James L. Snyder

Pulled from A.W. Tozer's sermons, this book captures his teaching on God's will for your life. We all face tough decisions, but Tozer's biblical insight will help guide you on the right path. In the same way that God led his people out of Egypt into the Promised Land, this book will help reveal where God is leading and reassure you that he is by your side.

A Cloud by Day, a Fire by Night

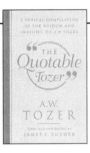

Enjoy the collected wisdom of one of the most beloved Christian authors in history with this seminal guide, ideal for fans, pastors, ministry leaders, and Christian writers. Arranged topically, this quick reference will open your eyes to the depth and insight of Tozer's thoughts on popular culture, the nature of God, spiritual warfare, God's Word, and more.

The Quotable Tozer

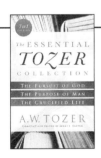

This 3-in-1 collection of A.W. Tozer's writings will strengthen your walk with Jesus. *The Pursuit of God* is sure to resonate if you long for a life spent in God's presence. *The Purpose of Man* is a call to worship as God reprioritizes your life and fills your soul. *The Crucified Life* will lead you to the cross so you can be raised to new life in Christ.

The Essential Tozer Collection

◆ BETHANYHOUSE

Stay up to date on your favorite books and authors with our free e-newsletters. Sign up today at bethanyhouse.com.

 facebook.com/BHPnonfiction   @bethany_house_nonfiction

 @bethany_house

You May Also Like . . .

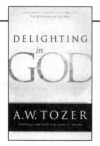

This follow-up to *The Knowledge of the Holy* expounds on Tozer's thoughtful insights and delves deeper into how the attributes of God—the things God has revealed about himself—are a way to understand the Christian life of worship and service.

Delighting in God

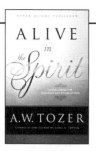

Though every Christian has the Holy Spirit, not every Christian is *filled* with the Spirit. Tozer explains the difference and how, if we use the gifts of the Spirit with wisdom and humility, the evangelical church can become what it was meant to be—and change the world.

Alive in the Spirit

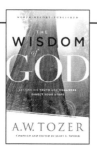

This powerful book captures Tozer's teachings on wisdom as a way to understand the well-lived Christian life. God's wisdom is a part of His character, and knowing this wisdom means drawing closer to Him.

The Wisdom of God

BETHANYHOUSE